I Wonder Why
Big Book
of
Knowledge

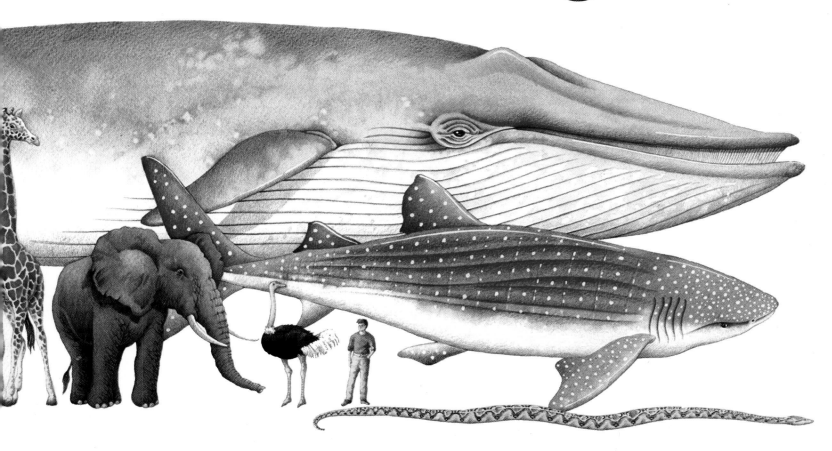

KINGFISHER

KINGFISHER

Kingfisher Publications Plc
New Penderel House
283–288 High Holborn
London WC1V 7HZ
www.kingfisherpub.com

Material in this edition previously published by
Kingfisher Publications Plc in the *I Wonder Why* series.

First published by Kingfisher Publications Plc 2005
10 9 8 7 6 5 4 3 2 1

1TR/0605/TIMS/RNB(RNB)/126.6MA/F

A CIP catalogue record for this book is available
from the British Library

ISBN-13: 978 0 7534 1187 2
ISBN-10: 0 7534 1187 3

Printed in China

CONTENTS

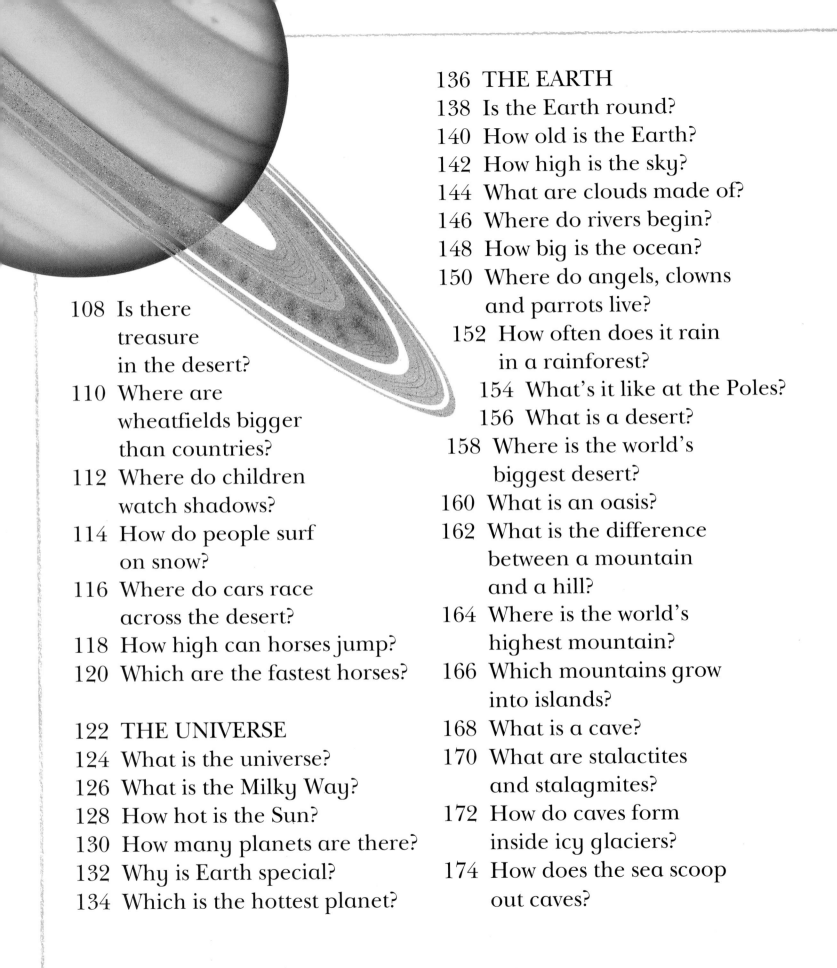

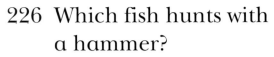

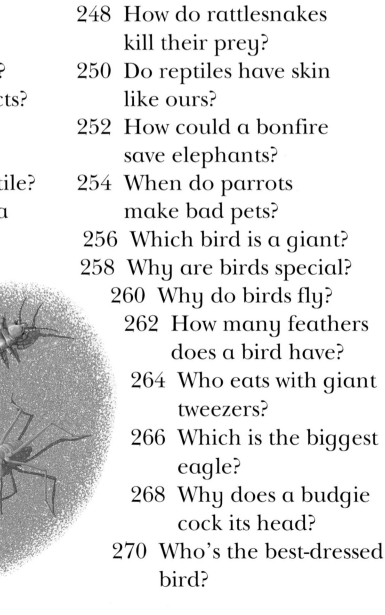

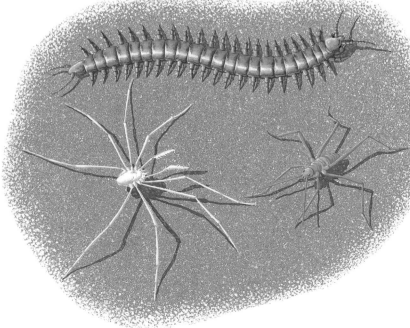

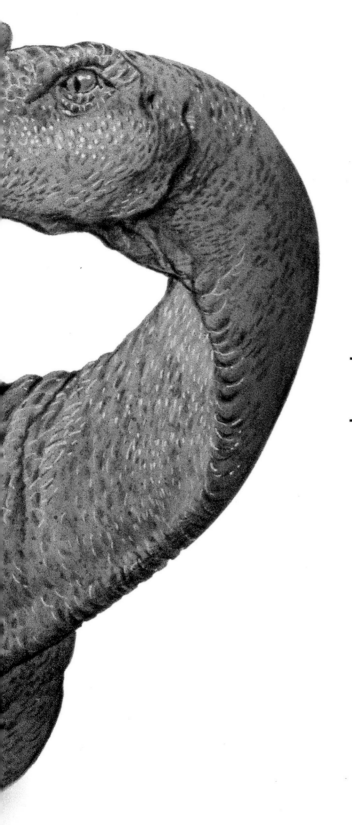

Prehistory

What is prehistory?

Prehistory is the time before people began to record in writing the things that happened to them and in the world around them. It is the story of Earth from its birth to the invention of writing, about 5,500 years ago.

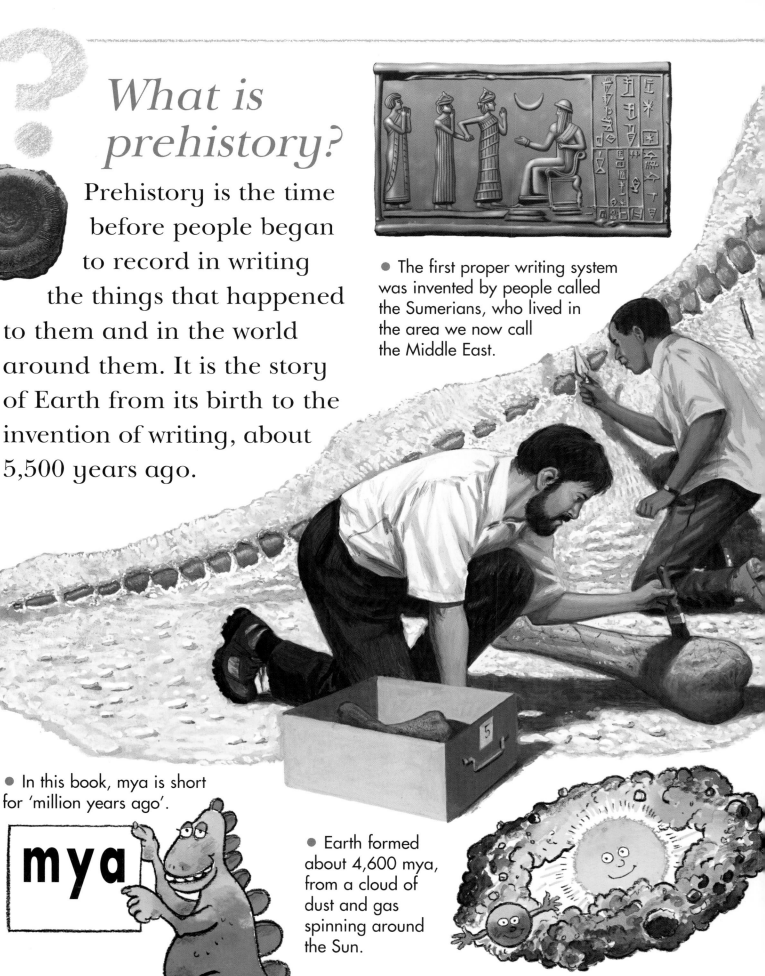

● The first proper writing system was invented by people called the Sumerians, who lived in the area we now call the Middle East.

● In this book, mya is short for 'million years ago'.

mya

● Earth formed about 4,600 mya, from a cloud of dust and gas spinning around the Sun.

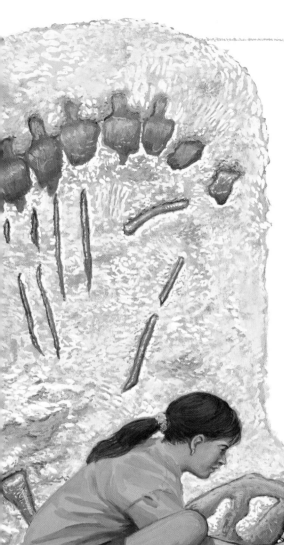

- Before the scientific study of fossils began in the late 1700s, some people thought fossils were real animals that had been turned into stone by hot sunlight.

How do we know about prehistoric life?

People who study prehistoric life work like detectives, slowly piecing clues together from fossils – the stony remains of animals and plants that died millions of years ago.

- Most fossils formed after a dead plant or animal sank to the bottom of a river, lake or sea, and was covered by layers of sand or mud.

- Over millions of years, the sand and mud hardened into rock, with the animal or plant buried inside as a stony fossil.

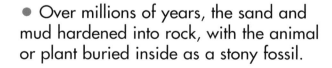

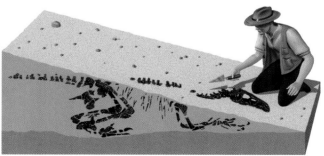

When did life on Earth begin?

Earth was a boiling hot mass of rock at first. Millions of years passed before its surface cooled down enough for life to survive. The first living things may have appeared as long as 4,000 mya, but so far scientists have not found fossils to prove this. The earliest-known fossils belong to microscopically tiny bacteria which lived in the oceans about 3,500 mya.

● The first many-celled creatures looked a bit like worms, jellyfish and sea anemones. Their bodies were soft and squishy, without bones or shells.

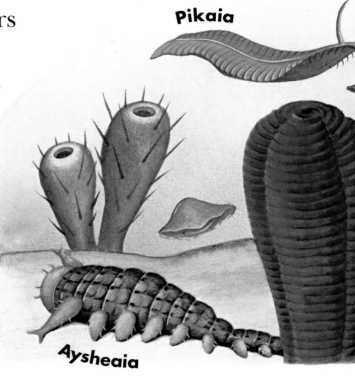

Pikaia

Aysheaia

● In some places the bacteria clustered together into mat-like sheets, which built up into mounds called stromatolites. Over time, the stromatolites became fossils.

Stromatolites

What is evolution?

Evolution is what scientists call the gradual change of one kind of living thing into another.

It happens very, very slowly. The first bacteria were tiny single cells. It took more than 2,500 million years for the earliest-known larger creatures, with bodies made up of many cells, to evolve.

Eldonia

Hallucigenia

● Dickinsonia was as wide as a swimming ring – it measured 60 centimetres across.

What is extinction?

Not all living things carry on evolving. Sometimes, a particular kind of animal or plant dies out and disappears from Earth completely. This is extinction.

● Trilobites evolved at least 600 mya, and became extinct about 240 mya. They were among the first animals to have eyes, and they were some of the earliest to have bodies protected by a tough shell-like exoskeleton.

Trilobite

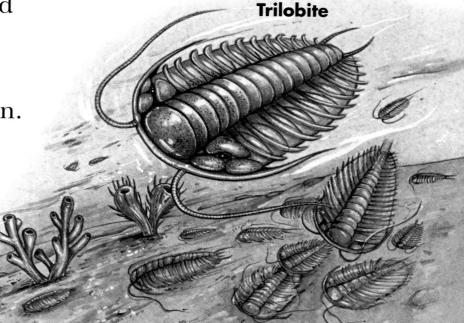

When did fish appear in the oceans?

When fish evolved about 500 mya, they were the first animals to have proper backbones. They had no jaws or fins, however, and looked rather like modern-day tadpoles.

Sacabambaspis

Climatius

Cladoselache

- With no jaws for biting or chewing, early fish like Arandaspis fed by hoovering up tiny creatures from the seabed.

Cheirolepis

- Dunkleosteus was a whopping six metres long, but it wasn't a shark. This scary monster belonged to a group called the armoured fish, because of the bony plates that protected their heads from attackers' teeth.

Dunkleosteus

Were sharks around in prehistoric times?

They certainly were – sharks were cruising the oceans by about 400 mya. They were among the earliest of the backboned animals to develop jaws and hard teeth, and they were just as ferocious as today's sharks!

● You wouldn't want to go swimming with Stethacanthus. The top of this early shark's weird T-shaped fin was covered in teethlike bristles, and so was its head.

What were the sea scorpions?

The sea scorpions were fierce hunters with barbed claws for snatching up their food. They lived at the same time as the early sharks and grew to two metres long. They did not have a backbone. Instead, their bodies were covered by a shell-like exoskeleton.

Pterygotus

When did plants get a foothold on land?

Plants were successful on land before animals, and the earliest-known fossils of a land plant date back to about 420 mya. Scientists call the plant Cooksonia, and it was tiny – about as tall as your little finger.

● Although Cooksonia had a stem, it didn't have leaves, flowers or proper roots.

Protocarus

Diplopodan

Why were prehistoric plants important?

The arrival of land plants meant that there was enough food around for land animals to evolve too. Among the first to eat up their greens were tiny mites, and insects such as springtails.

● All animals need oxygen to survive. Because plants use the Sun's energy to turn carbon dioxide into oxygen, they helped to bump up the air's oxygen levels.

- Once plant-eating land animals were around, meat-eaters evolved to munch on them.

Mesaraneus

Why did fish pop their heads above water?

Most fish take oxygen from the water through their gills. But after land plants appeared, something weird happened – some kinds of fish developed lungs for breathing air. Scientists call them lungfish, and think they evolved because there wasn't enough oxygen in the shallow rivers and lakes where they lived.

- The weather became much warmer at the time that lungfish evolved. Water evaporated and turned into gas, making lakes and rivers shallower, with less oxygen.

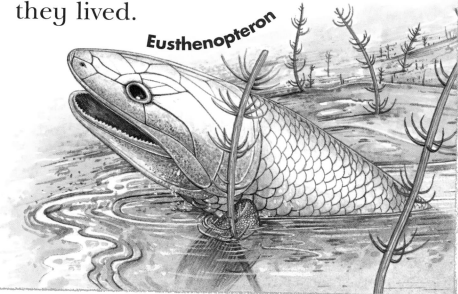

Eusthenopteron

Why did fish grow legs?

Some fish didn't just grow lungs, their fins became legs and they evolved into land animals! The earliest four-legged animals, Acanthostega and Ichthyostega, appeared about 370 mya. They spent most of their time in the water, but they could crawl about on land.

● Acanthostega and Ichthyostega were ancestors of the amphibians – animals that can live on land, but which lay their eggs in water.

Ichthyostega

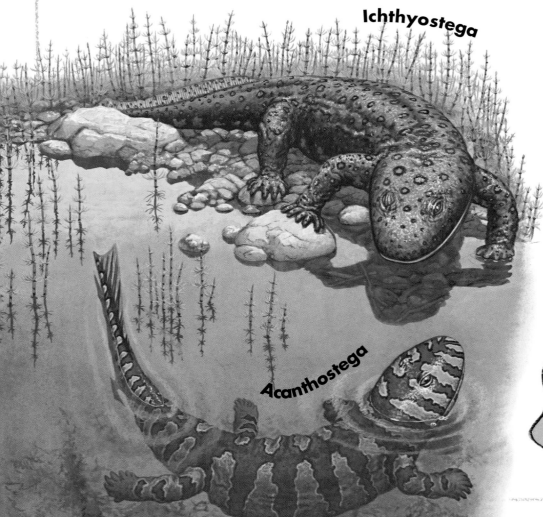

Acanthostega

● Diplocaulus was a bizarre early amphibian with a boomerang-shaped head. It lived mainly underwater, where its head worked like a submarine's hydrofoils.

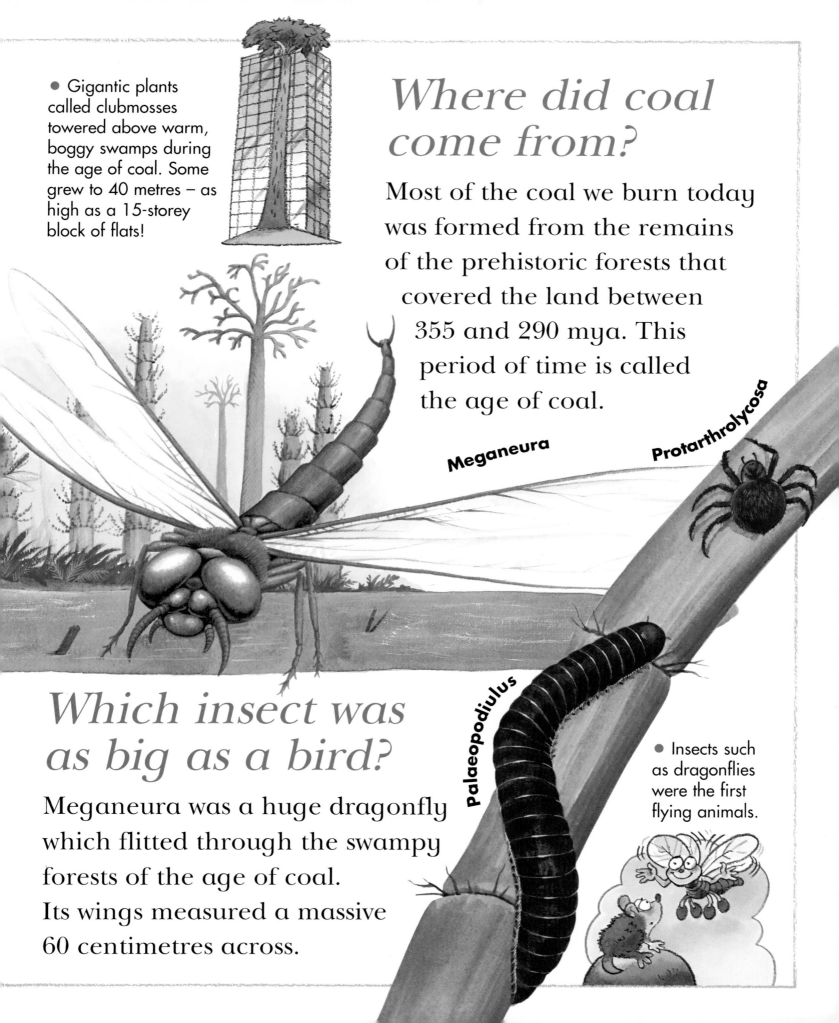

• Gigantic plants called clubmosses towered above warm, boggy swamps during the age of coal. Some grew to 40 metres – as high as a 15-storey block of flats!

Where did coal come from?

Most of the coal we burn today was formed from the remains of the prehistoric forests that covered the land between 355 and 290 mya. This period of time is called the age of coal.

Meganeura

Protarthrolycosa

Palaeopodiulus

Which insect was as big as a bird?

Meganeura was a huge dragonfly which flitted through the swampy forests of the age of coal. Its wings measured a massive 60 centimetres across.

• Insects such as dragonflies were the first flying animals.

When did reptiles appear?

Reptiles were a new group of animals which evolved from amphibians towards the end of the age of coal. Reptiles such as Hylonomus were the first four-legged animals to live in dry places where there was little water.

Hylonomus

● Reptiles have dry scaly skin, and their eggs don't dry out because each egg is protected by a leathery shell.

● Amphibian eggs have no shells, so they have to be laid in water to stop them drying out.

Which animals grew sails?

It isn't hard to work out how sailbacks like Dimetrodon got their name! Their sail-like fin probably worked rather like a solar panel, soaking up the Sun's heat.

● The sailbacks were reptiles, and reptiles are sunbathers. They love the Sun because they are cold-blooded – they cannot keep their blood warm without the Sun's heat.

Dimetrodon

Cynognathus

Which were the first furry animals?

Hair helps to keep animals warm, so most warm-blooded animals have furry or feathery coats. Scientists think the first warm-blooded furry animals were a type of reptile called the cynodonts, which evolved about 250 mya.

Did dinosaurs rule the skies?

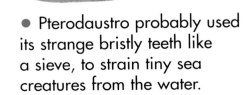

The dinosaurs did not have wings for flying. Other kinds of reptile called pterosaurs ruled the skies in dinosaur times. Pterosaurs came in all shapes and sizes, but they all had wings. Quetzalcoatlus was the biggest – its 12-metre wingspan made it the size of a small aircraft.

● Pterodaustro probably used its strange bristly teeth like a sieve, to strain tiny sea creatures from the water.

Quetzalcoatlus

Rhamphorhynchus

● Scientists have found fossils that show some pterosaurs had furry bodies, like modern-day bats.

Peloneustes

● Like land reptiles, the sea reptiles breathed air. Most of them had to return to land to lay their eggs.

Elasmosaurus

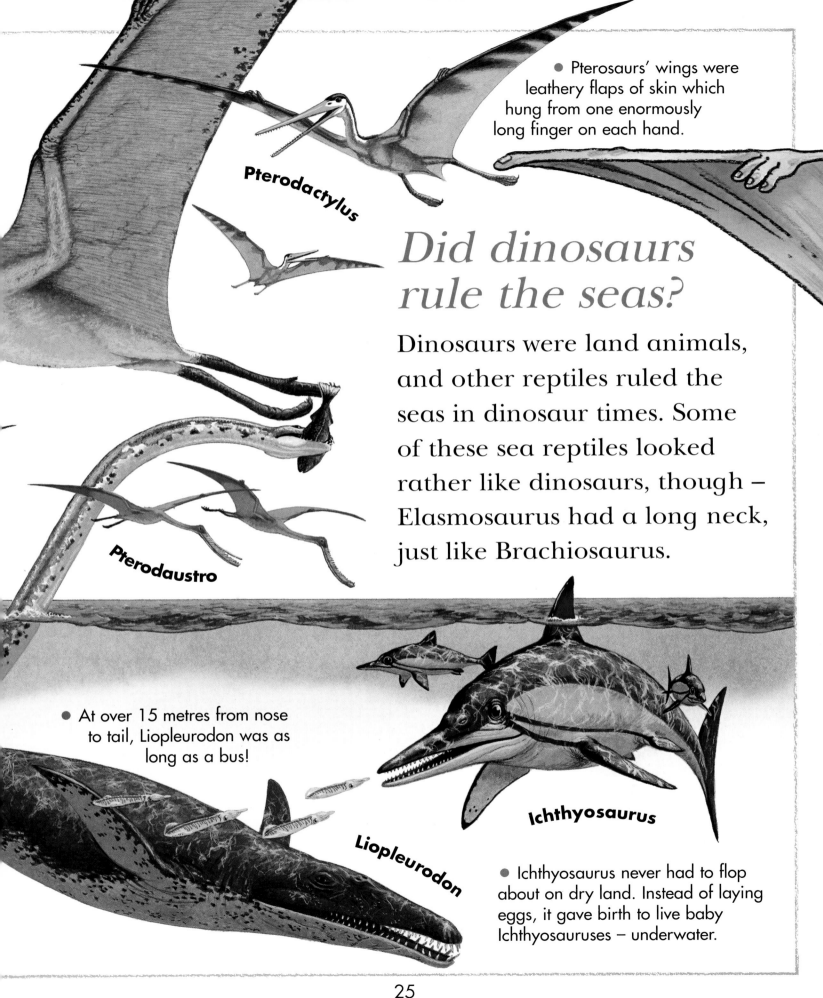

● Pterosaurs' wings were leathery flaps of skin which hung from one enormously long finger on each hand.

Pterodactylus

Pterodaustro

Did dinosaurs rule the seas?

Dinosaurs were land animals, and other reptiles ruled the seas in dinosaur times. Some of these sea reptiles looked rather like dinosaurs, though – Elasmosaurus had a long neck, just like Brachiosaurus.

● At over 15 metres from nose to tail, Liopleurodon was as long as a bus!

Liopleurodon

Ichthyosaurus

● Ichthyosaurus never had to flop about on dry land. Instead of laying eggs, it gave birth to live baby Ichthyosauruses – underwater.

Where did birds come from?

Dinosaurs may not have been able to fly, but scientists think that birds evolved from dinosaurs, and not from pterosaurs. The earliest-known feathered flyer was Archaeopteryx. It lived over 145 mya and scientists think it was a dinobird – half-dinosaur and half-bird.

Archaeopteryx

● Caudipteryx was another feathered dinobird, but it couldn't fly – its wings were too small.

● The duckbilled dinosaurs were gentle plant-eaters that came along after flowering plants appeared.

Edmontosaurus

When did the first flowers bloom?

Flowering plants didn't appear until about 140 mya, so only the later kinds of dinosaur would have seen and smelled them. Two of the earliest trees to blossom and fruit were magnolias and figs.

- Fossil-hunters have found part of a meat-eating dinosaur bigger than Tyrannosaurus. They've called it Giganotosaurus, which means 'giant southern lizard'.

Why was Tyrannosaurus king of the dinosaurs?

Imagine a giant with teeth as long as your hands and a mouth that's big enough to swallow you whole – that was Tyrannosaurus. It was one of the largest meat-eating land animals the world has ever known, and that's why it is called king of the dinosaurs.

Tyrannosaurus

- Tyrannosaurus was among the last kinds of dinosaur to evolve, fewer than 70 mya. Its name means 'tyrant lizard' (a tyrant is a cruel ruler).

Were mammals around in dinosaur times?

The first mammals had probably evolved from cynodonts by about 220 mya, a few million years after the first dinosaurs appeared. The earliest mammals were furry insect-eaters, not much bigger than modern-day mice.

Megazostrodon

Kamptobaator

Taeniolabis

Ptilodus

Zalambdalestes

● Megazostrodon could have sat on your hand – from its nose to the tip of its tail it only measured 12 centimetres.

● One of the special things about mammals is that mothers make milk in their bodies for their babies to feed on.

● The babies of most of the mammals living today develop in their mother's womb. They aren't born until they're big enough to survive in the outside world.

Which babies lived in their mother's pocket?

Early mammals laid eggs, as their ancestors the reptiles had done. Over time though, other mammals evolved. These gave birth to their babies, instead of hatching them from eggs. Marsupials first appeared about 100 mya. Marsupials are mammals whose newborn babies grow up in a pocket-like pouch on their mother's tummy.

Deltatheridium

● Newborn marsupials are no bigger than a jelly baby! They live in their mother's pouch until they are able to find their own food outside the pouch.

How do we know the dinosaurs died out?

Fossil-hunters haven't found anything to show that even a single lonely dinosaur has been alive during the past 65 million years – no fossil dinosaur bones, no fossil dinosaur footprints, nothing. All of the dinosaurs vanished 65 mya, along with all the pterosaurs and most of the sea reptiles.

Scientists haven't found dinosaur fossils in rocks that formed after 65 mya.

● Well over half of all the different kinds of animal on Earth became extinct 65 mya. No large animals seem to have survived beyond this time.

• We cannot be sure that it was the space rock that changed Earth's weather and killed off the dinosaurs. Some scientists think that exploding volcanoes sent up dust clouds to block out the Sun.

What killed the dinosaurs?

Many scientists think that the dinosaurs were wiped out after a city-sized chunk of space rock crashed into the Earth 65 mya. The impact was like tens of thousands of bombs exploding. Huge waves swept across the oceans and the land. Vast clouds of dust flew up into the sky, blotting out the Sun and plummeting Earth into icy darkness.

• Plants cannot grow without sunlight, so the big plant-eating animals died of cold and hunger first, and then the big meat-eaters.

• Some people used to think that the dinosaurs died out because the mammals ate all their eggs!

• No one knows for sure why some animals survived and others didn't. Perhaps it was because they were small enough to hide in burrows.

Which animals took over from the dinosaurs?

With no meat-eating dinosaurs around to hunt them, more and more new kinds of mammal began to evolve. Most were land animals, but some took to the air and others to the seas.

Icaronycteris

● Bats are flying mammals. One of the earliest-known bats was Icaronycteris, which appeared about 54 mya.

Smilodectes

Uintatherium

Hoplophoneus

Stylinodon

● Anancus had a hard time holding up its head. This early elephant's huge tusks were almost as long as the rest of its body.

● Whales are sea mammals which evolved at about the same time as bats. The earliest-known whale, Pakicetus, looked more like an otter than the whales of today.

Pakicetus

32

When were elephants as small as pigs?

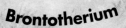
● When horses appeared about 50 mya, they were tiny, too. Hyracotherium had toes instead of hooves, and was cat-sized – about 20 centimetres high.

Elephants went through all sorts of weird and wonderful stages before they evolved into the animals we know today. When Moeritherium appeared about 40 mya, it was one of the earliest elephants – and only 60 centimetres high!

Moeritherium

Indricotherium

Brontotherium

Protocerus

Hoplophoneus

Which cats had dagger-sized teeth?

The sabre-toothed cats were named because of their massive fangs. These weren't used for eating, but for stabbing and killing their victims!

Who was Lucy?

● Lucy's fossilized skeleton was found in Africa in 1974. She was named after a Beatles' song, 'Lucy in the sky with diamonds', which was playing on the fossil-hunters' radio at the time.

Around 4.5 mya, some new mammals appeared on the scene – the earliest human-like creatures. They have scientific names such as Australopithecus, which means 'southern ape'. It's a bit of a mouthful, though, so it's easier to use nick-names, such as Lucy.

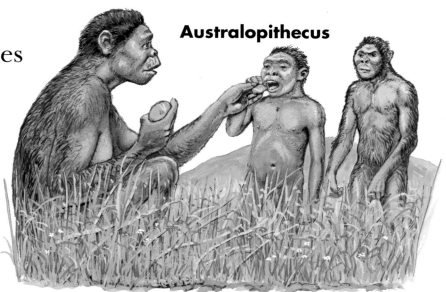

Australopithecus

Homo habilis

When did humans get handy?

Homo habilis means 'handy human', and these human ancestors were named because they were probably the first to use tools. They lived about two mya, and their tools were simple stone pebbles.

Who were the first explorers?

Although all early humans evolved in Africa, Homo erectus, who appeared about 1.9 mya, were very adventurous people. They were the first to head north out of Africa and explore Asia and Europe.

Homo erectus

● Homo erectus means 'upright human'.

● Homo sapiens were the first Australians. They sailed there from southeast Asia more than 50,000 years ago.

Who were the wise humans?

Modern humans are clever, which is why our scientific name is Homo sapiens, meaning 'wise human'. Our closest ancestors, the first Homo sapiens, evolved in Africa almost 200,000 years ago.

Homo sapiens

What were the Ice Ages?

The Ice Ages were long periods of time when it was so cold that snow and ice spread down from the North Pole to cover vast areas of Europe, Asia and North America. The Ice Ages began about 2 mya, and the last one melted away after the weather began warming up again about 12,000 years ago.

● Mammoths lived in northern lands, where their woolly coats kept them warm. The climate got too hot for them after the last Ice Age ended, and they became extinct.

Did Ice Age people live in caves?

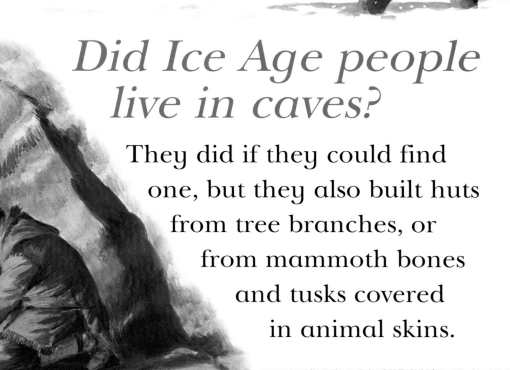

They did if they could find one, but they also built huts from tree branches, or from mammoth bones and tusks covered in animal skins.

The first crops were wheat and barley, and the first farm animals were goats and sheep.

Who were the first farmers?

Farming began about 10,000 years ago, when people in the Middle East began saving the seeds of wild plants to sow as their own crops. Growing their own food meant that farmers could stay in the same place all year round. They built villages, which grew into towns, and then into cities. Prehistory was over and, with the invention of writing, modern human history had begun.

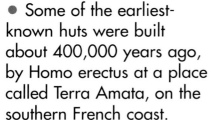

● Some of the earliest-known huts were built about 400,000 years ago, by Homo erectus at a place called Terra Amata, on the southern French coast.

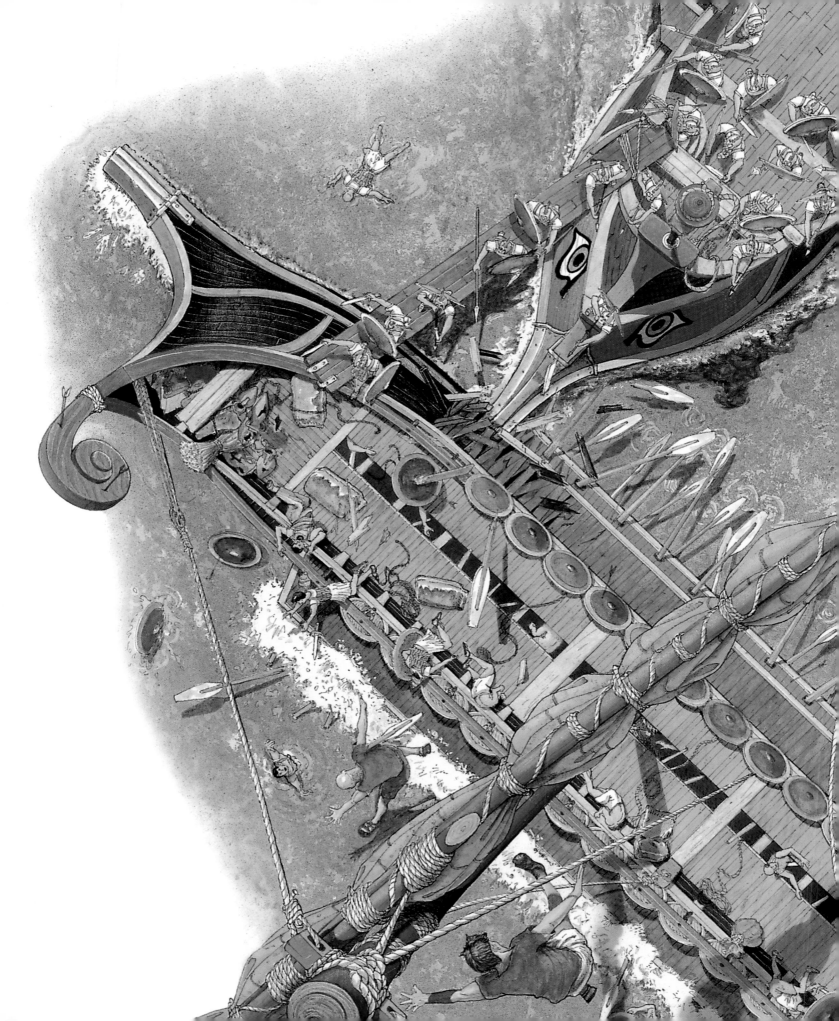

Ancient Civilizations

Why do we call Egyptians ancient?

Egypt — AFRICA

We call the Egyptians ancient because they lived such a long time ago – not because they all reached a ripe old age! The first Egyptians were farmers about 8,000 years ago. Within a few thousand years, Egypt had become one of the most powerful countries in the world.

● Will people be studying us in 5,000 years' time? What will they think about the way we live now?

● The Egyptians usually built tombs for dead kings on the river's western bank, where the Sun sets. They believed that their kings went to meet the Sun god when they died.

● Egypt is mostly sandy desert, where nothing grows. The Ancient Egyptians settled on the banks of the river Nile, where there was plenty of water for themselves and their crops.

● The Ancient Egyptians didn't know about distant parts of the world. But they did explore parts of Asia and Africa. And their merchants bought wood, gold, ivory, spices and even apes from nearby countries.

Why were the Egyptians great?

The Egyptians were so good at farming that they became very rich. They built fantastic temples for their gods, and huge pointed tombs called pyramids where they buried their kings. They had armies and ships and courts of law. Their priests studied the stars and their craftspeople made beautiful things from gold and silver.

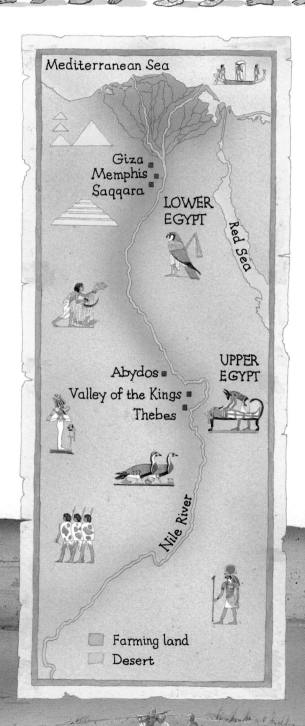

Mediterranean Sea

Giza
Memphis
Saqqara

LOWER EGYPT

Red Sea

Abydos
Valley of the Kings
Thebes

UPPER EGYPT

Nile River

Farming land
Desert

Who ruled Egypt?

The king of Egypt was called the pharaoh. The Egyptians believed that their Sun god Re was the first king of Egypt, and that all the pharaohs after him were his relatives. This made the pharaoh very holy – and very powerful! The people thought he was a god on Earth.

● The pharaoh's advisors were called the Honoured Ones. There were all sorts of royal officials, too, with grand names like the Director of Royal Dress and the Keeper of the Royal Wigs.

Could a woman be pharaoh?

Although very few women ruled Egypt, there was a famous pharaoh called Hatshepsut. When her six-year-old nephew came to the throne, Hatshepsut was asked to rule Egypt for him – just until he was a little bit older. But Hatshepsut liked ruling so much that she wouldn't let her nephew take over. He didn't get the chance to rule until he was 30 years old!

● When she was pharaoh, Hatshepsut had to wear the badges of royalty. These included a false beard, made of real hair.

How would you know if you met a pharaoh?

He would be wearing a crown, of course! In fact, pharaohs sometimes wore two crowns at the same time – a white one for Upper Egypt, which was the name for the south of the country, and a red one for Lower Egypt, which was the north.

Who was the crocodile god?

In old paintings and carvings, most Egyptian gods and goddesses have animal heads. The water god, Sebek, was shown as a crocodile. Thoth had the head of a bird called an ibis, while Taweret looked like a hippo! Osiris and Isis were luckier. They were shown as a great king and queen.

● The Egyptians loved to wear lucky charms. Their favourites were scarabs. The scarab beetle was sacred to the Sun god, Re.

● The Ancient Egyptians worshipped as many as 2,000 gods and goddesses!

Thoth, god of learning

Osiris, god of death

Who was the goddess Nut?

Nut was goddess of the heavens and she was usually shown covered in stars. Many gods and goddesses were linked in families. Nut was married to Geb. Isis and Osiris were their children.

● Being a priest was a part-time job. Most only spent 3 months a year at the temple, and lived at home the rest of the time.

● Priests had to wash twice during the day and twice at night, to make themselves clean and pure for the gods.

Taweret, goddess of childbirth and babies

Isis, wife of Osiris

Why did the Egyptians bury their mummies?

A mummy is a dead body which has been dried out so it lasts for thousands of years. The Egyptians believed that the dead travelled to another world, where they needed their bodies. And they didn't want any bits missing!

● Some poorer families had their nearest and dearest mummified, but it was an expensive business. Only the rich could afford a really good send-off.

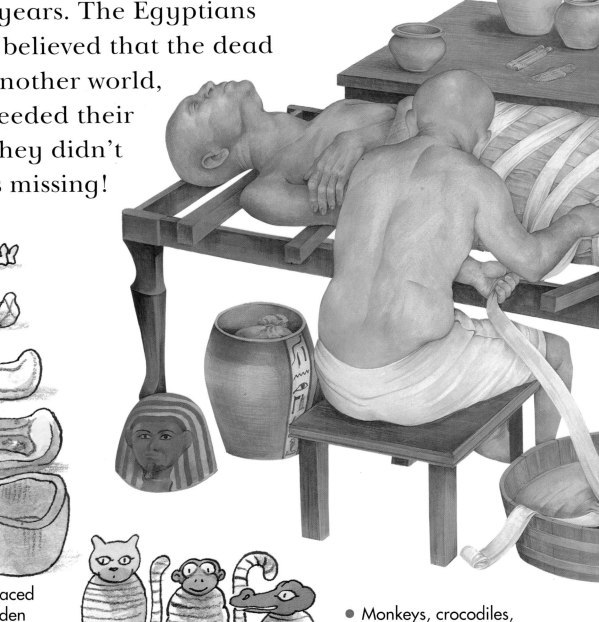

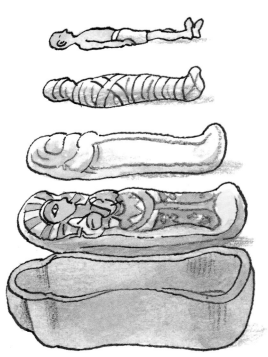

● The mummy was placed inside a series of wooden coffins. These were put in a big stone case called a sarcophagus.

● Monkeys, crocodiles, cats and other sacred animals were often mummified, too!

Why were mummies brainless?

The Ancient Egyptians believed that the heart was the most important part of the whole body. They thought that the brain was useless. So when they were preparing a mummy, they took out the brain – by pulling it down through the nose!

Why were mummies wrapped in bandages?

Wrapping the dead body helped to keep its shape. After the insides were removed, the body was dried out for 40 days in salty stuff called natron. Then it was washed, rubbed with ointments, and tightly bandaged.

Why were the pyramids built?

The pyramids were huge tombs for dead pharaohs and other very important people. No one knows exactly why the pyramids were shaped this way. Some people think they were built to point towards the Sun and stars, so that the dead person's spirit could fly to heaven like a rocket.

● The Great Pyramid at Giza was built more than 4,500 years ago. This is what it looks like today.

● Pharaohs were buried with all their finest clothes and jewellery, so tombs were given sneaky traps to catch out robbers.

● There are other, smaller pyramids at Giza, and over 80 at other places in Egypt. Some have stepped sides and bent tops.

48

● This is what the Great Pyramid looks like inside.

Pharaoh's chamber

Who were the Ancient Greeks?

The Ancient Greeks were people who lived in Greece from around 3,500 years ago. But they didn't live only in Greece. Some lived to the north and the east, in lands that we now call Bulgaria and Turkey. Others lived on small rocky islands in the Aegean Sea.

● Many Greek people set sail for North Africa, Turkey, Italy and France. They found safe harbours, where they built new homes and towns, and cleared the land for farming.

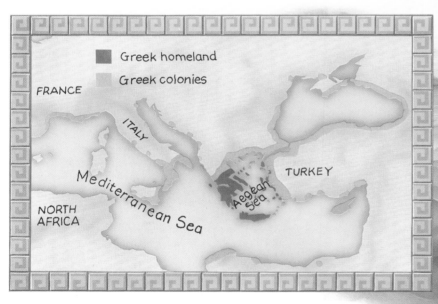

Greek homeland
Greek colonies
FRANCE
ITALY
Mediterranean Sea
NORTH AFRICA
Aegean Sea
TURKEY

● By 500BC the Greek world was large, rich and powerful. It stretched from France in the west to Turkey in the east.

● Wherever they went, the Greek settlers took their own way of life. They must have looked odd to the locals!

● The Greeks were a talented people. They had good laws and strong armies. They built beautiful temples and theatres. And they were great thinkers, artists and athletes.

Why did Greece grow bigger and bigger?

Greece and its homelands were small, and much of its land was too rocky for farming. By about 750BC, there was little room left for new towns or farms, and food began to run short. Because of this, many people left Greece to look for new places to live, and the Greek world began to grow.

Was Greece one big happy country?

Ancient Greece was not a single country like Greece is today. It was made up of different states, which were cut off from each other by high mountains, deep valleys, or the sea. The states weren't much bigger than cities, but they each had their own laws and army, and often quarrelled with each other. Athens was the biggest city-state.

● Each state was made up of a city and the surrounding countryside. Many city-states lay close to the sea, and had a harbour, too.

HARBOUR

TEMPLE

PRISON

SCHOOL

AGORA

CITY WALLS

FARMLAND

Where did the citizens take charge?

• Sparta was a city-state in southern Greece. It was ruled by two kings from two royal families, who were helped by a council of wise old men.

THEATRE

HOUSES

In Athens, all grown men who weren't slaves were citizens. They could choose their government officials and vote for or against new laws. Citizens could also speak at the Assembly. This was a huge open-air meeting where people stood up and told the government what it should be doing.

• There had to be at least 6,000 citizens at every Assembly. They all met on the slopes of a hill in Athens, and voted by raising their hand.

Where did the clock go drip-drop?

• Most wealthy Greek households had slaves. The slaves did all the hard work, such as building, farming, housework and looking after the children.

Citizens who spoke at the Assembly weren't allowed to drone on for too long. Each speaker was timed with a water clock. When the last drop of water had dripped out of the jar, his time was up. He had to sit down and hold his tongue!

Who was goddess of wisdom?

Athene was the goddess of war and also of wisdom, and so her symbol was the wise owl. She had special powers to protect the city of Athens. Because of this, the citizens loved and worshipped her. They built Athene her very own temple, the Parthenon, high on the Acropolis, a hill overlooking the city.

● According to stories, the gods lived on top of Mount Olympus, the highest mountain in Greece. But they didn't always behave as you'd expect gods to – they spent a lot of their time quarrelling!

Hermes messenger of the gods

Zeus king of the gods

Demeter goddess of crops

Aphrodite goddess of love and beauty

Hera queen of the gods, goddess of women and children

Hades god of the underworld

● The Greeks believed in many different gods and goddesses. Each one had different powers. Some of the gods were kind, but others were stern and cruel.

Who told stories about the gods?

A famous poet called Homer told many exciting stories about gods and heroes. His long poem *The Odyssey* tells the adventures of Odysseus, a Greek soldier sailing home to Ithaca from the war with Troy. The sea god Poseidon tries to sink his ship, but with Athene's protection, Odysseus finally gets home.

● Poseidon was god of the sea. He tried to sink Odysseus's ship by stirring up violent storms.

● Inside the Parthenon stood a towering statue of Athene – about ten times taller than you! It was covered with precious gold and ivory.

Why did actors wear masks?

In Ancient Greece, only boys and men were actors. They wore masks so that the audience could see what part they were playing – a man or a woman, a wise person or a fool. Greek theatres were huge, with seats for up to 17,000 people. From the back you couldn't have seen the actors' faces, but the big, colourful masks were easy to make out.

● Greek theatres stood on sloping hillsides. Their semicircular shape helped carry the actors' voices right to the back – even when they whispered!

● Some plays lasted all day. The audience took cushions and rugs to put on the hard stone seats, and bought snacks and wine when they felt hungry or thirsty.

How did a tortoise make music?

Sad to say, a tortoise only made music when it was dead. An empty tortoiseshell was used to make a lyre, a musical instrument rather like a harp. Musicians fixed strings to the shell and plucked them to play a tune.

● The double flute was another popular musical instrument but it was difficult to play. You needed twice as much puff as for a single flute, and each hand played a different tune.

● Theatre staff carried big sticks in case of trouble. Sometimes the huge audience got carried away by a play and began to riot. A few hefty whacks soon quietened them down!

Why were the Olympics held?

The Olympic Games were part of a religious festival in honour of Zeus, king of the gods. Every four years, 20,000 people flocked to Olympia to watch athletes run, box, wrestle, and race chariots. The hardest event of all was the pentathlon. Contestants had to take part in five different sports – the long jump, running, wrestling, throwing the discus and throwing the javelin.

● Women were banned from the Olympics. They held their own games, in honour of Hera, queen of the gods. The women's games had only one event, which was running.

● At the Olympics all the athletes were naked. The Greeks were proud of their bodies, and weren't afraid to show them off!

Did the winners get medals?

Winning at the Olympics was a great honour, just as it is today. But there were no medals in the ancient games. Instead, the winners got crowns made of laurel leaves, jars of olive oil, beautiful pots or vases, and pieces of wool, silk or linen to make into clothes.

● Greek boxers didn't wear padded gloves like boxers today. They simply wrapped strips of leather around their fists.

Who ran the first marathon?

In 490BC the Greeks won a battle at Marathon, about 42 kilometres from Athens. A Greek soldier called Pheidippides ran all the way to Athens to tell the citizens the good news. Sadly, his 'marathon' exhausted him, and the poor man collapsed and died.

● There was no marathon race in the ancient games, but there is today. It measures 42 kilometres – exactly the same distance that poor Pheidippides ran 2,500 years ago.

Who were the Romans?

The Romans were people who came from Rome. About 2,000 years ago they became so powerful that they began to conquer the lands around them. By AD100 they ruled a huge empire, and were one of the mightiest peoples in the ancient world.

● Different parts of the empire had very different climates. Romans boiled in Egypt, where the summers were sweltering...

● An old legend says that the city of Rome was first started by a man called Romulus. He and his twin brother Remus had been abandoned by their parents and looked after by a wolf!

BRITAIN

Hadrian's Wall

London

FRANCE (Gaul)
•Lyon

Alps

SPAIN

Pyrenees

ITALY

•Rome

Pompeii

Carthage

AFRICA

Did all the Romans live in Rome?

● ...but they shivered in the icy Swiss Alps and in northern Britain. These were the coldest places in the whole empire.

The city of Rome wasn't big enough for all the Romans! All in all, there were about 50 million people in the empire, which stretched from Britain in the north to Africa in the south. Everyone in the empire was protected by Rome's armies, but had to obey Rome's laws.

THE ROMAN EMPIRE AD100

Caspian Sea

Black Sea

Constantinople

ASIA MINOR

Athens • Ephesus
• Antioch

SYRIA

Mediterranean Sea

ARABIA

N

Alexandria

EGYPT

Red Sea

● It would have taken nearly 100 days to ride from one end of the empire to the other. It was a journey of over 3,000 Roman miles, about 5,000 kilometres.

3,000 miles

Who ruled Rome?

Over the years, Rome was ruled in three different ways: first by kings, then by a number of officials who were chosen by the people, and finally by emperors, who were really kings under a different name!

● Some Roman emperors ruled wisely, but others did whatever they pleased…

Nero was mad and bad. Some people say he set fire to the city of Rome.

Hadrian visited every corner of the empire, and made it stronger.

Caligula wasted the riches of Rome. He believed he was a god.

Who was born free?

Roman citizens. They were not only able to vote in elections, they also got free seats at the amphitheatre and free use of the public baths. When times were hard, they got free loaves of bread, too!

- Roman women did not have the same rights as men. They were not allowed to vote, and had to obey their husband or father. But that doesn't mean they always did!

Who slaved away for the Romans?

Most of the hard work in Rome was done by slaves. These men, women and children were captured abroad, and then sold in the marketplace in Rome. They had to wear an identity tag with their master's name and address on it – just in case they got lost.

- The first Roman emperor was called Augustus. He was advised by a group of wealthy men, called senators, who were used to running the army and the government.

- Slaves were sometimes given their freedom after many years of good service, or if their master wanted to be kind.

VII

When did the army use tortoises?

When Roman soldiers were advancing towards the enemy, they did a special trick called 'the tortoise'. They held their shields high above their heads to make a sort of shell. This protected them from enemy spears – but made it hard for them to see where they were going!

Dear Mum
ıv/vıı/cıv
Having an awful time.
The Barbarians are fierce and I think the Centurion hates me.
Please send X sesterces for food.
Your loving son
Marcus × × ×

● Soldiers were often hungry and cold. Many of them wrote letters home asking for extra food and clothing.

● Injured soldiers bandaged their wounds with cobwebs soaked in vinegar. This helped the soldiers, but wasn't so good for the spiders!

Which soldiers left home for 25 years?

Most soldiers had to stay in the army for 25 years. Those who were Roman citizens were luckier – they could leave after just 20 years! Soldiers had a hard life. They were far from home, and had to put up with danger, tough training and harsh punishments.

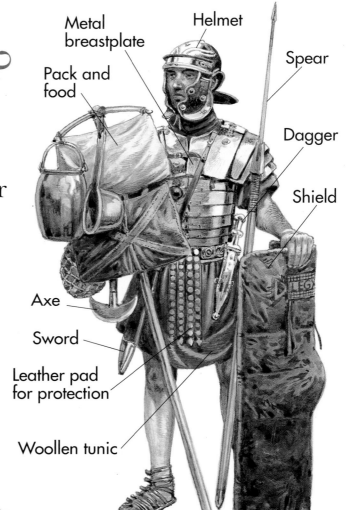

Metal breastplate
Helmet
Pack and food
Spear
Dagger
Shield
Axe
Sword
Leather pad for protection
Woollen tunic
Leather sandals

● In warmer parts of the empire, soldiers didn't wear much under their tunics. But in chilly places they wore thick woollen underpants – just like the locals.

Who did the Romans worship?

The Romans worshipped hundreds of different gods and goddesses. They believed that the gods watched over them night and day. Some looked after the earth and the sea. Some cared for special groups such as doctors, merchants or soldiers. And others watched over the different parts of people's lives – their health, beauty or love life.

● The Romans thought that snakes brought good luck, so they painted them on their walls.

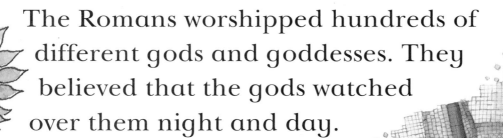

Mars, god of war

● The Romans believed that spirits lived in the rivers, woods and fields. They protected wild animals and the plants that grew there.

Venus, goddess of love

Juno, queen of the gods

Neptune, god of the sea

• Sick Romans prayed to the gods to cure them. If they got better, they left a thank-you present in the temple – a little statue of the part of their body that had been cured.

Diana, goddess of the Moon and of hunting

Apollo, god of the Sun and of the arts

• The Romans built temples as homes for the gods. Each god or goddess had a temple of their own. It was built in the finest stone, and decorated with statues and carvings.

XIII

Who was thrown to the lions?

● The amphitheatre in Rome was the Colosseum. It could seat up to 50,000 spectators.

On special days, people flocked to see spectacular shows at the amphitheatre. Christians, criminals and slaves were thrown into a ring with lions, and were chased, wounded and killed. The crowds cheered noisily. They thought it was fun to watch people suffer – but to us it seems wicked and cruel.

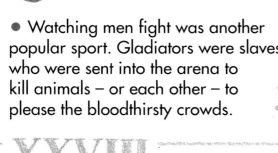

● Watching men fight was another popular sport. Gladiators were slaves who were sent into the arena to kill animals – or each other – to please the bloodthirsty crowds.

• Lions, leopards, crocodiles, wolves and bears – many different kinds of animal were shipped to Rome from all over the empire. Thousands were killed in the amphitheatre in a single day.

Were there hippos in the hippodrome?

The hippodrome, or circus, was a huge sports stadium with an oval-shaped racetrack. There were no hippos, but there were exciting chariot races. This was the Romans' favourite sport, and huge crowds filled the hippodrome to bet on their favourite teams.

XXIX

Why were Roman roads so straight?

The Romans were brilliant engineers. Before they built a road, they used measuring instruments to work out where the road should go. They chose the shortest, straightest route between two camps, forts, or towns – and got rid of any hedges, buildings or other obstacles in the way. The roads linked the whole empire.

PLAN VIEW

SIDE ELEVATION

ARCHITECT
Marcu

● Road-builders put milestones along the side of the road so that travellers knew how far they had gone. A Roman mile was 1,000 paces long, about 1.6 kilometres.

ROME
500
MILES

● The roads had strong foundations. On the bottom, a thick layer of sand was covered first by stones, and then by gravel. On the top was a smooth surface of carefully-fitted paving stones.

Which bridges were always full of water?

Aqueducts look rather like bridges, but instead of a pathway along the top they have a deep channel of water. The Romans built them to carry water from mountain streams to nearby cities. Without aqueducts, the people wouldn't have had their baths, toilets or fountains of fresh running water.

CLAUDIUS
EMPEROR

ippa II

● The Romans invented concrete by mixing lime, water and the ash from volcanoes. Concrete was as strong as stone, and it set hard even under water.

● The Romans invented arches, too. Each arch rested on a wooden frame until the very last stone, called the keystone, was in place.

The
Middle
Ages

What were the Middle Ages in the middle of?

We call the years between the ancient world and the modern world in Europe the Middle Ages. They started in the 470s, when rule by the Romans came to an end, and they finished in the 1450s.

● The Romans once ruled most of Europe and North Africa. Then fierce warriors invaded, splitting Roman lands into many small kingdoms. By the 1450s Europe had larger countries again, more like those of today.

NORTH AMERICA

IROQUOIS

ANASAZI

Pueblo Bonito

Newfoundland

ATLANTIC OCEAN

MAYA

AZTECS

PACIFIC OCEAN

SOUTH AMERICA

INCAS

● The map above includes the people and places talked about in this book.

● In the Middle Ages, no one knew what the whole world looked like.

74

VIKINGS

A S I A

EUROPE
• Venice

MONGOLS

JAPAN

PERSIA

CHINA
• Leshan

Mediterranean
Sea

• Fez

INDIA

Angkor
• Wat

ARABIA

Timbuktu •
AFRICA
Ife •

Great •
Zimbabwe

INDIAN

OCEAN

AUSTRALIA

NEW ZEALAND

MAORIS

● This is what Arab map-makers thought the world looked like in the 1150s. It shows Asia, North Africa and Europe. Neither the Arabs nor the Europeans knew about other parts of the world.

● Most people thought the world was flat. Sailors were afraid of falling over the edge if they went on long voyages!

Why did kings and queens wear crowns?

Rulers had much more power in the Middle Ages than they do today. They made the laws, and everyone had to do what they said. A glittering golden crown was like a badge – it was one way of showing how important the king or queen was.

- In many countries today, laws are made by the group of people we call a parliament, not the king or queen.

Barons and bishops

King and queen

Freemen and women

Knights

Peasants

- The king told the barons what to do. The barons told the knights what to do. Everyone told the poor peasants what to do.

- The ruler of the Inca people of South America was called the Sapa Inca. His crown was made of gold and feathers. His tunic and cloak were made of fine wool.

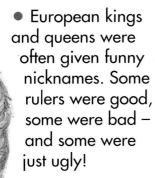

Why were the peasants revolting?

Well, they didn't actually look revolting, just a bit muddy! Poor people often rose up in revolt and fought against their rulers, though. They were trying to win a better way of life.

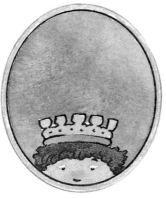

- The peasants had to give money or food to their local lord every year – even though they often went hungry themselves.

- European kings and queens were often given funny nicknames. Some rulers were good, some were bad – and some were just ugly!

Malcolm the Bighead
King of Scotland

Wladislaw the Short
King of Poland

Emanuel the Happy
King of Portugal

Why did knights wear armour?

In battle, knights were bashed and battered about by swords, arrows, axes, long pointed lances and metal clubs called maces. They had to protect their bodies from all these sharp weapons, so they wore suits of tough metal armour.

● Until the 1200s most knights wore chain-mail armour. This was made from linked metal rings. Later armour was made from solid metal plates.

By the end of the Middle Ages, a knight was like a can of beans on legs – completely covered in metal!

● Putting on armour wasn't easy. A squire was a boy who was learning to be a knight. He helped the knight get ready for battle.

Armour wasn't very comfortable to wear, so knights put on thick padded clothes underneath.

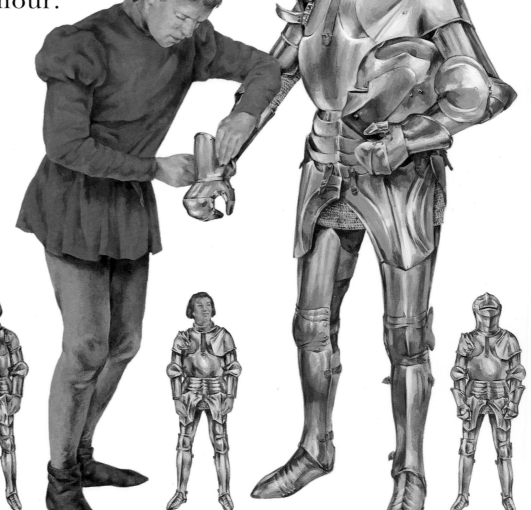

● Japanese knights were called samurai. Their armour was made of metal plates fixed to padded silk and leather.

● Bows and deadly arrows were used by soldiers in most parts of the world.

Welsh longbowman

Turkish crossbowman

Aztec warrior

Mongol archer

● A samurai always had a bath before going into battle. Then, if he died, he knew he would be clean and ready to go to heaven.

Where did china come from?

From China, of course! Pottery was made all over the world, but the very finest was invented in southern China. It is called porcelain.

● It was probably a Venetian workman making glass windows who discovered that pieces of glass could help people with poor eyesight to see better.

Who got puffed in Venice?

Venice was famous for its glass, which is made by melting sand and other materials. It is shaped while it is still hot and soft. Glass-blowers blow it up like a balloon, through a long iron tube.

80

• The Chimú people of South America used precious gold and turquoise to make this knife. Priests used it at ceremonies. In the 1400s, Chimú lands were taken over by the Incas.

• The Yoruba people were brilliant metal-workers who lived in the kingdom of Ife, in West Africa. This bronze sculpture was made in the 1300s and shows the head of a king.

Why did artists break eggs?

There weren't shops selling tubes of paint in the Middle Ages, so artists had to make their own. In Europe they made a kind of paint called tempera by mixing egg yolks and water into their colours.

Why were books chained up?

Books were rare because each one had to be written out slowly by hand – until the 1400s, there were no machines to print them quickly. This made the books very precious, so they were often chained up to stop people from stealing them.

● Monks made books, writing with goose quills dipped in ink. They spent many hours decorating each page, using bright colours and even tiny slivers of gold.

● The Chinese were the first people to print books rather than copy them out, about 1300 years ago. They used wooden blocks.

● In Europe, printing began when a German called Johann Gutenberg built a printing press in the 1440s. He used metal type blocks.

Why was it hard to tell the time?

There were clocks that told the time by drips of water, but they froze over in winter. There were candles that told the time as they slowly burned down, but they kept blowing out. And there were sundials that used shadows to tell the time – except when it was cloudy!

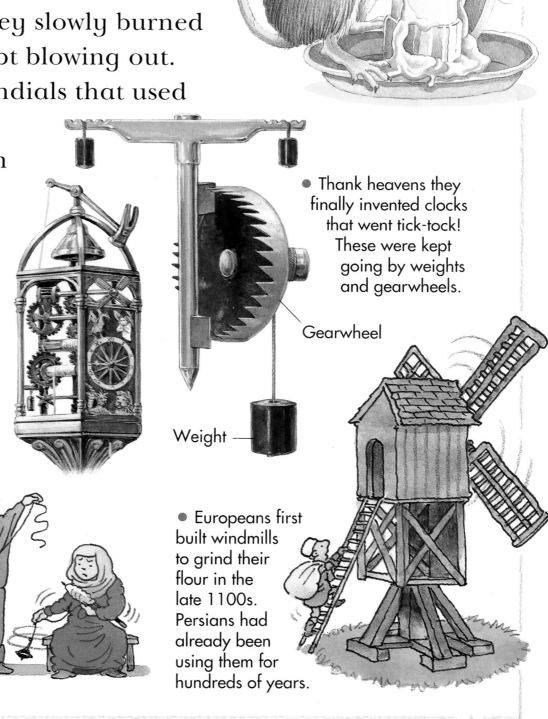

● Thank heavens they finally invented clocks that went tick-tock! These were kept going by weights and gearwheels.

Gearwheel

Weight

● Spinning wheels came to Europe from China and India in about 1200. Like all good inventions, they made life better – turning a wheel to spin thread was much easier and quicker than twiddling a spindle.

● Europeans first built windmills to grind their flour in the late 1100s. Persians had already been using them for hundreds of years.

Why did people eat with their fingers?

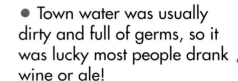

Although Europeans used knives and spoons at mealtimes, no one had forks. Rich and poor alike put pieces of food into their mouths with their fingers instead. At feasts, servants passed around fish and meat in handy chunks, so they were easy to pick up – if they weren't covered in slippery sauce!

- Town water was usually dirty and full of germs, so it was lucky most people drank wine or ale!

- It was good manners to throw left-over bones on to the floor for the dogs.

- A royal feast might end with a giant surprise pie. When the pie was opened, out would jump musicians or acrobats or strange animals.

- Until the 1400s, most people didn't eat off plates. They used a thick slice of bread called a trencher instead – sometimes finishing their meal by eating it.

● Poor peasants had little choice of food. Most ate dark bread made of rye or barley flour, porridge or vegetable stews.

Did people eat potatoes?

The Inca people of South America grew and ate potatoes, but until the 1500s no one else had ever seen a potato, let alone tasted one! Explorers took these and many other new vegetables to Europe from the Americas.

● The Incas kept a kind of guinea pig for food, just as farmers in other countries kept pigs. Guinea pigs are still eaten in Peru today.

Did people chew gum?

The Maya people of Central America chewed a rubbery gum they called chicle. They collected it from the sapodilla tree.

What were garderobes?

Castle toilets were called garderobes. They were usually built high up in the walls. Everything fell down into the moat, or into a stinky cesspit – which some unlucky servant had to clean out from time to time.

● There weren't many toilets in the Middle Ages. Most town people used pots, and just poured the smelly contents away into the street.

Did people take baths?

People around the world had different ideas about bathing, but Europeans weren't too keen on it at this time. People who had money could pay to visit a public bathhouse. Only the very rich had their own baths. They used wooden tubs, so they had to watch out for splinters!

● Southern Europeans started using soap in the 700s. It took a bit longer for northerners to start washing behind their ears!

This is what a plague flea looks like under a microscope.

What was the Black Death?

The Black Death was the kind of terrible sickness we call a plague. Within just 13 years, it killed at least one out of every three people in Asia and Europe. Whole families and villages were wiped out.

● The Black Death began in about 1338 and spread from Asia to Europe, carried by rats. The rats had tiny fleas, which passed the plague on when they bit people.

Who wore steeples on their heads?

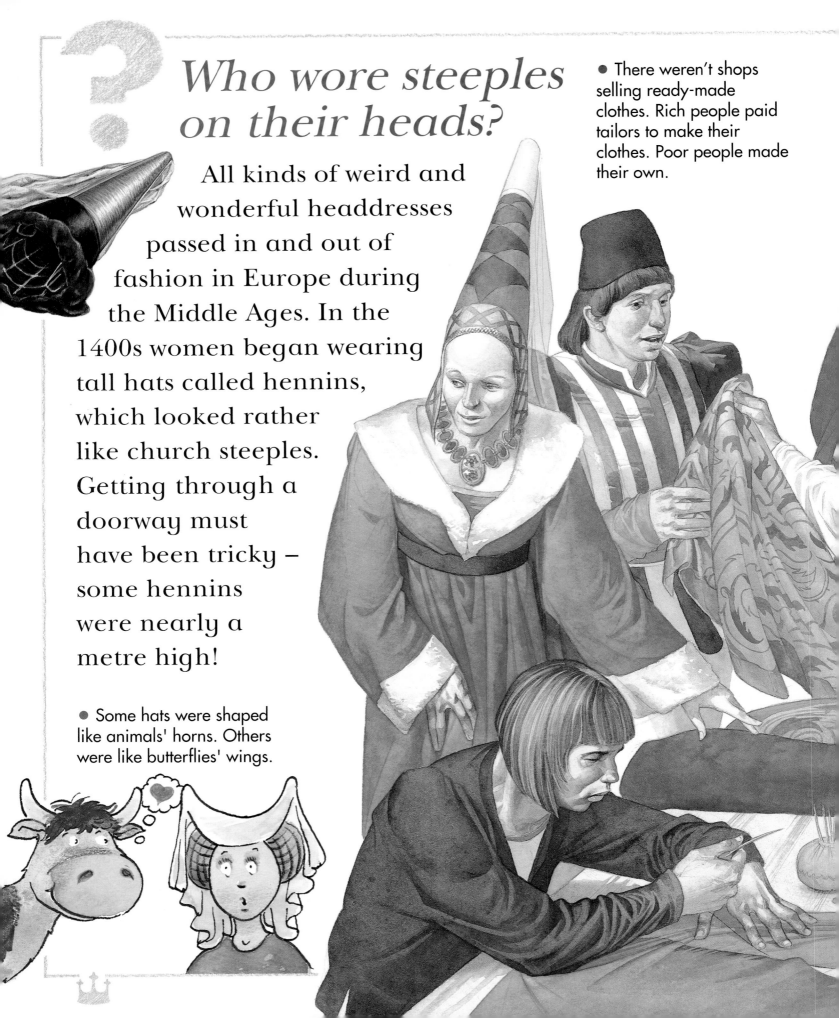

All kinds of weird and wonderful headdresses passed in and out of fashion in Europe during the Middle Ages. In the 1400s women began wearing tall hats called hennins, which looked rather like church steeples. Getting through a doorway must have been tricky – some hennins were nearly a metre high!

● Some hats were shaped like animals' horns. Others were like butterflies' wings.

● There weren't shops selling ready-made clothes. Rich people paid tailors to make their clothes. Poor people made their own.

● People showed off all their money by wearing expensive clothes and jewellery. The finest materials were made in Italy, Spain and the East.

● Some French knights trying to escape from an enemy army had to cut the points off their shoes before they could run away!

● Have you ever seen shoes with long pointed toes like this? The toes were so long they had to be tied to the wearer's leg! They were all the rage for men about 600 years ago.

Who wore platform shoes?

Streets were so muddy that noble ladies started to wear shoes with very high soles. Maids often had to hold the lady up as she walked along!

Why was football banned?

Football wasn't played by teams on a pitch in the Middle Ages – boys just chased the ball through the streets, yelling and kicking and knocking people over. By 1314, it had got so bad that King Edward II of England banned football in London.

● Footballs were made from pigs' bladders.

● The Aztecs and the Maya played a game called tlachtli, with a rubber ball on a stone court. It was a bit like basketball.

● Lacrosse was first played by the Iroquois people of North America. Games could last for hours, with as many as 1,000 people in each team!

What was the Festival of Fools?

The Festival of Fools was held in many parts of Europe around Christmas time. It was a kind of holiday, when ordinary people had fun pretending to be lords and priests, and doing all sorts of silly or naughty things.

Who said yes to Nō plays?

Nō are Japanese plays in which actors wear masks and move very slowly, telling story-poems through mime and dance. They were first performed in the 1300s, at the court of the Japanese emperor.

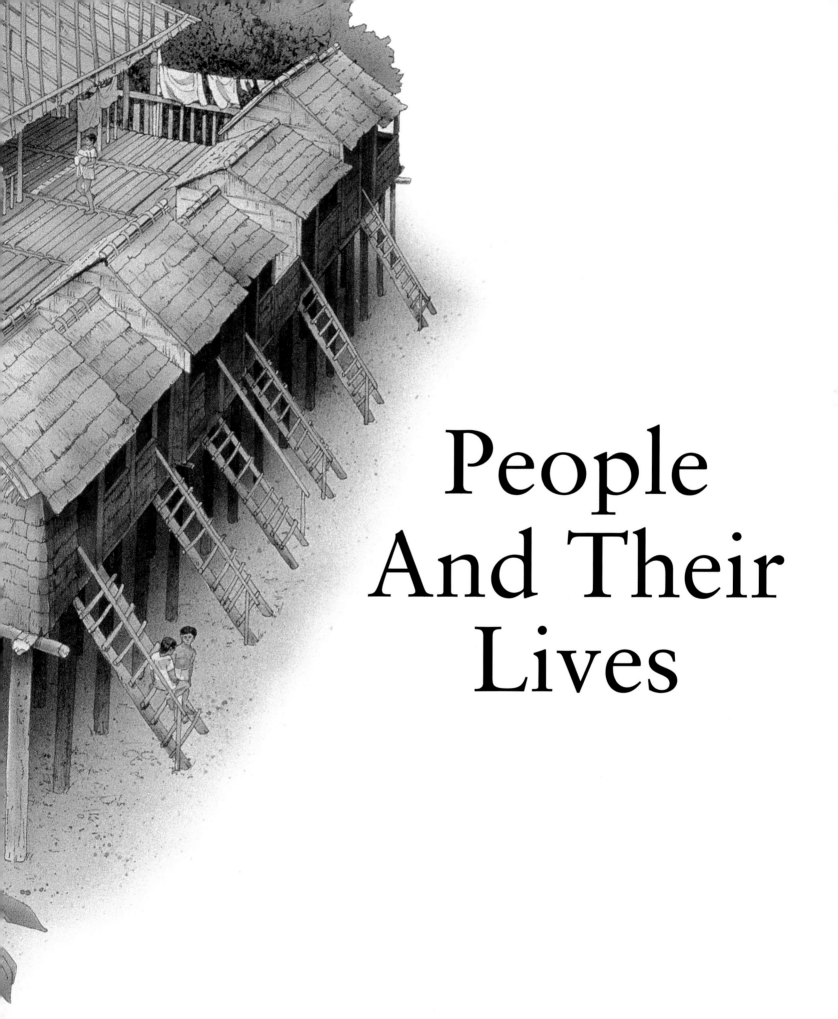

People
And Their
Lives

Do people live in caves today?

Yes, they do – either in natural caves, or in rooms they've dug out of the rock. In the Shanxi Province of northern China, for instance, millions of people live in cave homes. Some families even grow crops on their roofs.

● It's so hot during the summer that almost all buildings in the Australian mining town of Coober Pedy are underground. The town is a centre for opal mining, and around 2,500 people live there.

Where can you play sport in a cave?

In Norway's Gjøvik Rock Cavern, which was blasted from the rock to house a huge underground sports stadium where ice-hockey matches were held during the 1994 Winter Olympics. At 91 metres long and 61 metres wide, it's one of the world's largest artificial rock chambers.

● Saumur, in France's Loire Valley, is also famous for its cave homes. The caves were dug out in the 18th century by stonemasons, who used the stone to build the valley's great chateaux.

Why are caves good for cheese?

Caves are the key to one of France's tastiest cheeses – Roquefort. It is made from sheep's milk, and its special flavour comes from the streaks of blue-coloured mould. Moulds are fungi, like mushrooms, and they grow from seeds called spores. These are added to the sheep's milk in the early stages. The young cheeses are put in a network of caves, which provide the right climate for the spores to grow into mould.

● Cave conditions are also ideal for storing wine and for farming all kinds of edible mushroom.

How do people live in the desert?

Desert survival is all about finding enough water and food to stay alive. Some desert people move from place to place all the time, following good sources of water and food. These travelling people are called nomads.

● The San people of the Kalahari Desert are so expert at tracking down water, they can find small pockets of it under the sand. They suck up the water through a reed straw and store it in an ostrich shell.

What do nomadic people find to eat?

Few desert nomads hunt for wild food these days. Instead, most keep their own herds, so they can drink the animals' milk or make it into cheese.

Who ate ants?

In the past, the nomadic Aboriginal people of the Australian deserts survived entirely by hunting and finding wild food – everything from kangaroos to lizards, insects and plants. Sweet things were rare, so finding a nest of honeypot ants was an extra-special treat.

● When rains make the desert bloom, honeypot ants feed on sugary nectar from flowers. Some ants store the nectar in their bodies, turning themselves into living honeypots.

● The Tuareg are nomadic herders who live in the Sahara Desert. Their name means the 'people of the veil' – the men's faces are almost completely hidden by their veil-like turbans.

● Nomadic peoples do not move on every day – only when they need fresh supplies of water or food.

Why did Australian explorers import camels?

In February 1861, Robert Burke and William Wills became the first settlers to cross Australia from south to north. They wanted camels to carry their supplies because their route took them straight through the deserts in the continent's heart. But because camels aren't Australian animals, the explorers had to import them from Afghanistan.

Darwin

Burke and Wills die at Cooper Creek camp

Melbourne

● Sadly, Burke and Wills both starved to death on the return journey south. Their companion, John King, survived.

Who made it across the Sahara in a microlight?

British explorer Christina Dodwell did in the 1980s, during her mammoth 11,000 km flight across Africa. Her tiny flying machine was called *Pegasus*, after the winged horse of ancient Greek legend.

Which desert explorer carried water in his boots?

Swede Sven Hedin nearly died of thirst when he travelled across Asia's Taklimakan Desert in the 1890s. When he at last stumbled across water, two of his companions were dead and the third had given up walking hours before. Hedin saved the third man's life by carrying water back to him in his boots.

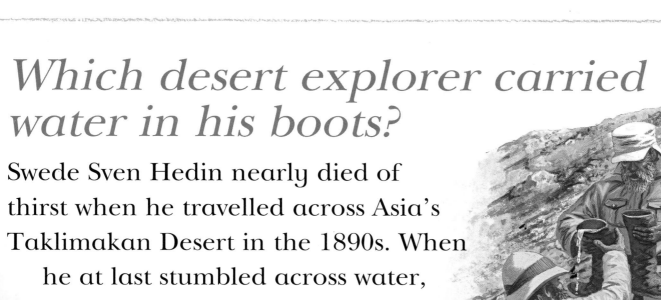

• When Chinese monk Hsuan Tsang set off alone into the Gobi Desert in the 600s, almost the first thing he did was to drop his waterbag. He was saved by his horse, which smelled grass growing around a waterhole and led him to safety.

Why do mountain houses have sloping roofs?

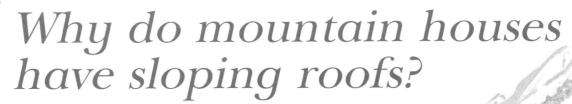

A sloping roof stops too much snow piling up on top of a mountain house – the extra snow slides off, like a skier sliding down a slope. The parts of the roof that stick out beyond the walls are very wide, too, to keep the falling snow away from the walls.

Why do farmers build steps on mountains?

In many parts of the world, mountain farmers build low walls to stop rainwater washing the soil away. This creates stepped fields called terraces, where the soil is deep enough for crops to grow.

- Lake Titicaca is too high for many trees to grow, so everything from boats to houses is made out of reeds.

- If you don't want to build a house on a mountain, you can always live a cave. Since earliest times, the people of Cappadocia, Turkey, have tunnelled homes in weird chimneys of volcanic rock.

Who fishes on the world's highest lake?

At 3,812 metres above sea level, Lake Titicaca in Peru, South America, is the highest navigable lake in the world. Local people live on islands in the lake and fish from boats woven from reeds.

- Some mountain rivers are blocked and turned into lakes by a strong high wall called a dam. The lake water is used to drive machines that generate electricity.

Who built palaces in the mountains?

Back in the 1400s, the Incas ruled over vast parts of the Andes Mountains of South America. They built amazing stone towns and palaces in the mountains, including the mysterious Machu Picchu.

● The Incas were conquered by Spanish invaders in the 1500s. When American explorer Hiram Bingham stumbled across Machu Picchu in 1911, it had been deserted for well over 400 years.

Which monks live in the mountains?

Mount Athos in Greece is home to 20 monasteries, and lots and lots of monks. It isn't a single peak. It is a mountainous strip of land that sticks out like a finger from the mainland.

Which city is on top of the world?

Tibet borders the Himalayas, and it's so high that people call it the 'roof of the world'. It's no surprise, then, that the Tibetan city of Lhasa is the world's highest, at 3,600 metres above sea level.

● Even valley bottoms in Tibet are higher than most countries' mountains.

● Women aren't allowed to visit Mount Athos – even female animals are banned!

Who were the mountain men?

American explorers like Kit Carson became known as mountain men during the 1800s, because they roamed through the wildest parts of the Rocky Mountains, trapping beaver and other animals for their fur.

Who lives in a longhouse?

On the tropical island of Borneo, some people live in long, airy buildings, which are made of wood and bamboo, and are raised on stilts. These longhouses are home to dozens of different families, each with their own room.

● As many as 100 families may share the same longhouse.

● Tower blocks are another way of squeezing a lot of homes into a small space. You find them in big towns and cities.

Where do gardens grow on rivers?

In the Netherlands, many people live on barges moored on the country's canals. Boat-owners don't have gardens, of course, but some of them grow flowers on the roof!

How do you keep cosy in the Gobi?

The Gobi Desert is in Mongolia in northern Asia and its winters are icy cold. Some shepherds and their families travel around the desert, living in thick, felt tents called yurts, which keep out the hot sun or the freezing cold.

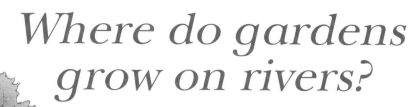

Could people live in space?

They already have! Some astronauts have lived in space stations spinning around the Earth for as long as a year. There are plans for much bigger stations, where people could live for 10 years, and even for settlements on Mars.

● It would take 8 months to reach Mars in a spacecraft. The crew would have to take everything they needed with them – the food for just one person would make a pile twice as big as a family car.

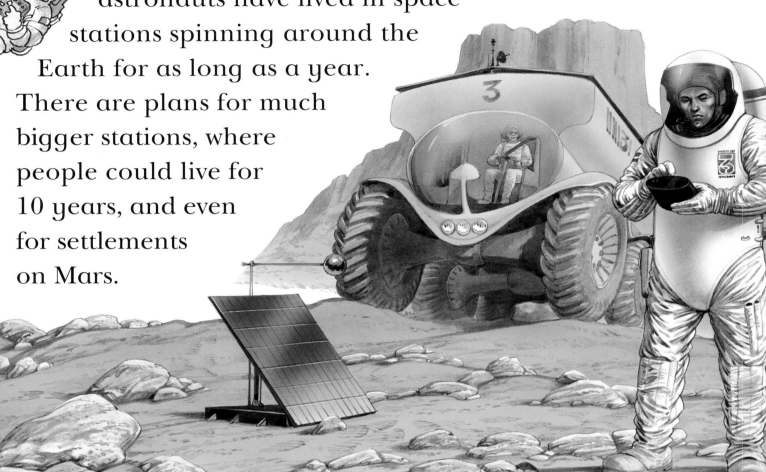

● There are plans for a huge wheel-shaped space station, measuring over 1 kilometre across.

● People have even lived under the sea, but not for longer than a few weeks at a time. They were working in underwater laboratories.

Could people live in a greenhouse?

They already have! In the USA's Arizona Desert there's a gigantic greenhouse called Biosphere II. It's like a miniature Earth, with its own farm, lake and stream, rainforest and desert – there's even a mini-ocean with a coral reef.

● Biosphere II is an experiment. The people who live inside it are completely cut off from the outside world. Scientists are studying whether people could live this way out in space.

Could people live underground?

They already do! In the Australian outback town of Coober Pedy, people dig holes to mine the precious gemstones called opals. They also carve out cool underground homes, to escape from the scorching heat up on the surface.

Is there treasure in the desert?

Yes – gold, silver and diamonds have all been found in deserts. One of the world's largest diamond mines is in the Kalahari Desert.

● Salt was as precious as gold in ancient times, and there were salt mines deep in the Sahara Desert.

What is black gold?

People often call oil 'black gold', because it's one of our planet's most valuable natural resources. Finding it on their land has made individual people and entire countries very, very wealthy.

● Much of the world's oil is drilled from rocks deep beneath the Arabian deserts.

How can deserts give us clean energy?

Solar power stations are places where the Sun's heat is used to generate electricity. They're much cleaner than a power station that burns oil or coal, and hot deserts are the ideal places to build them.

● The world's largest solar power station is in the USA's Mojave Desert.

Where are wheatfields bigger than countries?

The rolling grasslands of Canada and the USA are planted with wheat as far as the eye can see. One Canadian wheatfield was so big, it was double the size of the European country, San Marino!

● Huge combine harvesters have to work in teams to harvest the gigantic wheatfields.

● More people eat rice than wheat. Rice plants need to stand in water, and are grown on flooded land called paddy fields.

Where does chocolate grow on trees?

Chocolate is made from the seeds of the cacao tree. Sadly, the trees don't grow everywhere – just in the hot, wet parts of South America, southeast Asia and West Africa.

Which country has more sheep than people?

● In Thailand, coconut farmers train monkeys to harvest their crop. The monkeys scamper up the trunks of the palm trees and throw down the fruits.

Although there are more than 17 million people in Australia, most live around the coast. In the centre people run enormous sheep farms. At the last count, there were 147 million sheep – nearly nine times the number of people!

Where do children watch shadows?

Shadow puppet shows are enjoyed by people all over the world. On the Indonesian island of Java, the audience sits on both sides of a cloth screen. One side watches the puppets while the other sees the shadows dance, as if by magic!

● Javanese puppets are made of painted leather. The puppeteer moves them with wires or rods.

● In a Vietnamese water puppet show, the story is acted out on the surface of a lake. It can't be much fun for the puppeteers – they have to stand in the water.

Who makes pictures from sand?

The Navajo people of the southwestern United States create beautiful pictures with grains of coloured sand. The pictures are made on the ground for special ceremonies. But these works of art don't last long – they are destroyed afterwards!

● Some sand pictures are said to have healing powers and are large enough for someone ill to sit in the middle of them.

● In Switzerland, cow herders used to play alpenhorns – long wooden horns which echoed from one mountain to another.

Which dancers snap their fingers?

Flamenco dancing comes from southern Spain. Proud-looking dancers toss their heads and snap their fingers, as they stamp and whirl to the music of a Spanish guitar.

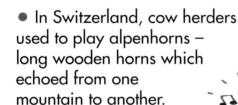

How do people surf on snow?

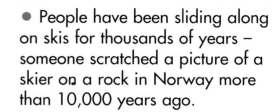

They head for the mountains with a snowboard! Snowboards are a cross between a ski, a surfboard and a wheel-less skateboard. When they were first made in the 1960s, they were called 'Snurfers'.

• People have been sliding along on skis for thousands of years – someone scratched a picture of a skier on a rock in Norway more than 10,000 years ago.

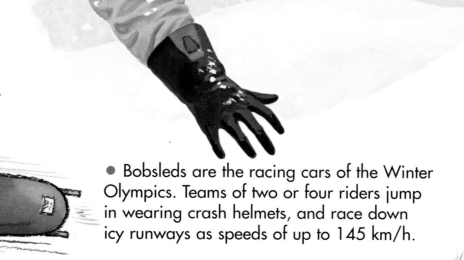

• Keen snowboarders don't give up when spring comes and the snow melts. They just switch to a new kind of souped-up skateboard – the mountainboard.

• Bobsleds are the racing cars of the Winter Olympics. Teams of two or four riders jump in wearing crash helmets, and race down icy runways as speeds of up to 145 km/h.

Who hurtles down mountains faster than an express train?

High-speed trains can zip along at over 200 km/h, and so can speed-skiers and snowboarders. Speed-skiers are the fastest – the world record is nearly 250 km/h.

Which bike climbs mountains?

A mountain bike has lots of gears to help you pedal up steep tracks, and knobbly tyres for gripping slippery slopes. And if the going gets too tough, you can always get off and carry the bike!

Where do cars race across the desert?

Briton Andy Green became the world's fastest man on wheels in October 1997, when his jet-propelled car *Thrust SSC* reached a mindboggling 1,227.9 km/h. He set the record on the smooth, flat surface of the USA's Black Rock Desert.

● In January every year, drivers dice with death racing through the Sahara Desert during the Paris to Dakar rally. In 1983, 40 drivers had to be rescued after losing their way during a terrible sandstorm.

Why are Space rovers tested in the desert?

● The *Sojourner* rover was tested in US deserts before its launch to Mars, where it landed in 1997.

Being in a desert is the nearest you can get on Earth to experiencing what it's like on Mars. And that makes a desert the ideal place for putting a Space rover through its paces.

Which is the world's toughest foot race?

You have to be made of tough stuff to enter the Marathon of the Sands. This foot race takes place in the Sahara Desert, with runners covering around 230 km in six days – that's further than five normal marathons!

● Although the temperature can reach 45°C at midday, the Saharan runners have to carry food, clothes and everything else they need – apart from a tent.

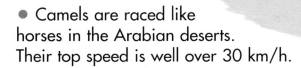

● Camels are raced like horses in the Arabian deserts. Their top speed is well over 30 km/h.

117

How high can horses jump?

● Walls are made of wooden bricks so the horse isn't hurt if it knocks them down.

The highest fences in a top-level showjumping competition can be two metres or more – taller than the horse! The aim of riding a showjumping course is to get around it without knocking down any of the fences.

Where do horses play games?

A gymkhana is a riding competition with mounted games for single riders and teams. With games like the sack race and flag race, it's rather like a school sports day!

● Winners and runners-up are awarded rosettes made from coloured ribbons.

What is dressage?

Dressage is a special series of movements designed to show how well a horse and its rider work together. The movements include riding in a circle, a figure of eight and a curved shape called a serpentine.

● Just about the toughest challenge for a horse and rider is eventing – a three-part competition covering dressage, showjumping and racing around a cross-country course.

● One of the trickiest dressage moves is the pirouette, in which the horse canters around in a circle without moving forwards.

FINISH

Which are the fastest horses?

Racehorses are the kings of speed. A galloping racehorse can pound around a course with a jockey on its back at over 60 kilometres per hour.

● Steeplechasing began in the 1750s in Ireland, when two riders decided to test their horses' speed by racing across country between two churches – chasing each other from steeple to steeple!

What is a steeplechase?

In a steeplechase, horses have to jump fences, ditches and other obstacles as they race around a course. A course without obstacles is a flat race.

Who sits in a sulky?

Jockeys do, for a sport called harness racing. A sulky is a modern-day mini-chariot, which is attached to the horse by tack called a harness. The jockey perches on a seat over the sulky's wheels, and guides the horse with extra-long reins.

● It doesn't matter on which day they were really born – all racehorses born in England have their official birthday on 1 January.

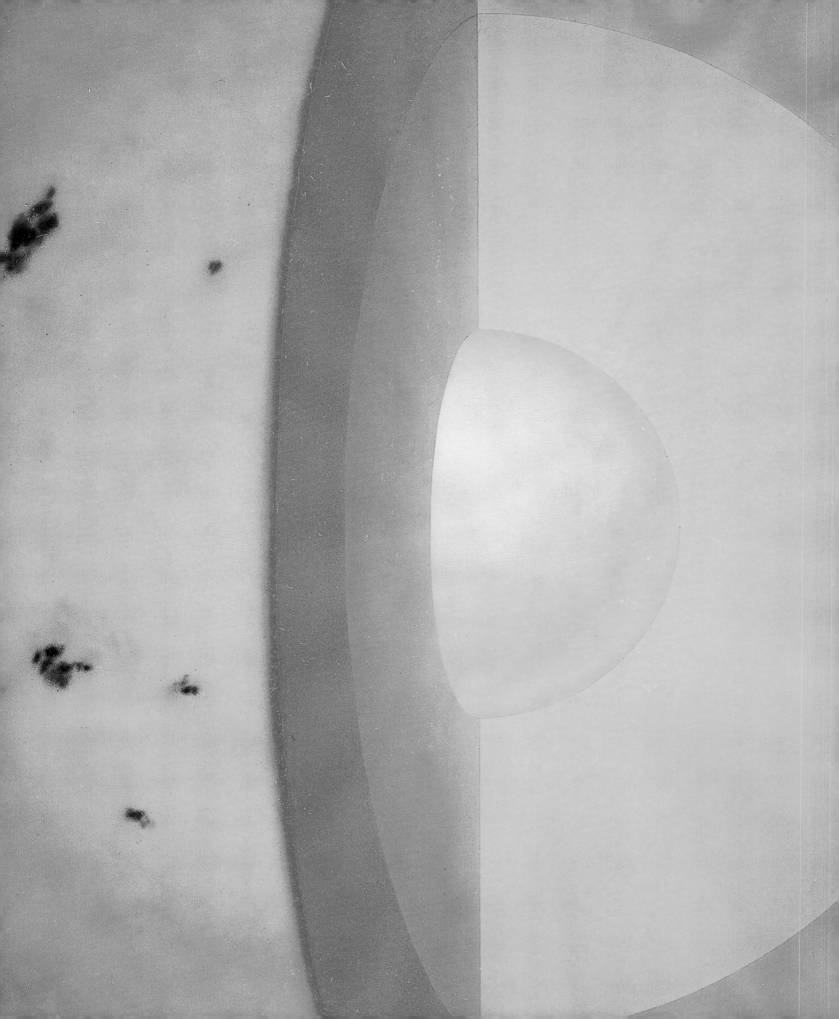

The
Universe

What is the universe?

The whole world and everything beyond it is the universe. It is all the stars and planets, the Earth and its plants and animals, you and me – everything.

- You are made of the same stuff as a star!

- There are huge groups of stars in space. They're called galaxies, and they're like gigantic star-cities.

- The Big Bang explosion sent the young universe flying out in all directions. Over vast ages of time, bits came together to make galaxies.

- The galaxies are still speeding apart today, and the universe is getting bigger.

When did it begin?

- To see how the universe is getting bigger, watch the spots as you blow up a spotty balloon.

Many astronomers think that everything in the universe was once packed together in one small lump. Then, about 15 billion years ago, there was a gigantic explosion which they call the Big Bang.

Will the universe ever end?

Some astronomers think the universe will just carry on getting bigger as the galaxies speed apart. Others think that the galaxies may one day start falling back towards each other until they crash together in a Big Crunch!

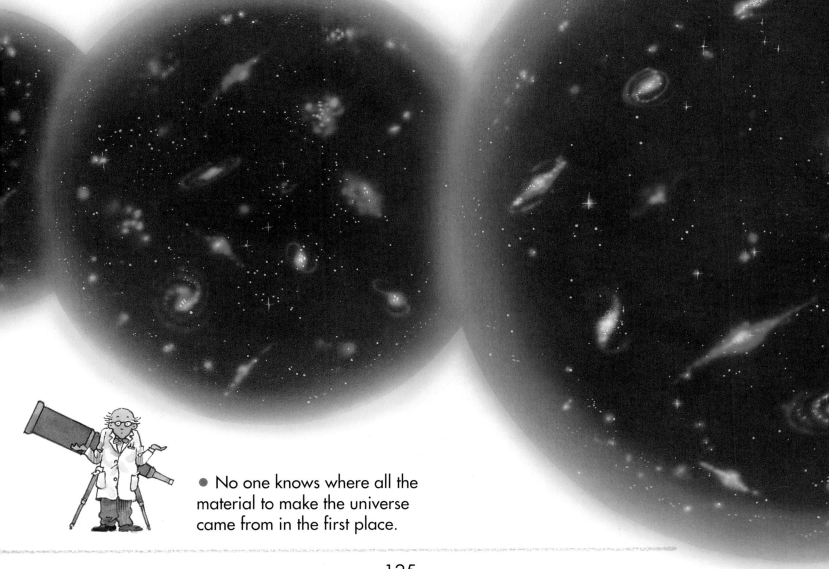

● Astronomers are scientists who study the stars and the planets.

● No one knows where all the material to make the universe came from in the first place.

What is the Milky Way?

The Milky Way is the galaxy we live in. It is made up of all the stars you can see in the sky at night, and lots and lots more you can't see.

● The Milky Way is a spiral galaxy. Below you can see what it looks like from above – a bit like a whirlpool with long spiralling arms.

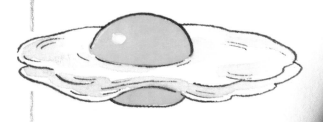

● From the side, a spiral galaxy looks like two fried eggs stuck together.

● The Milky Way got its name because at night we can sometimes see part of it looking like a band of milky white light across the sky.

● We live on a planet called Earth, which travels around a star called the Sun.

126

• Astronomers usually give galaxies numbers instead of names. Only a few have names that tell us what they look like – the Whirlpool, the Sombrero, and the Black Eye, for example!

• These are the three main galaxy shapes.

Irregular (no special shape)

Elliptical (egg-shaped)

Spiral

How many stars are there?

There are about 1000 billion stars in the Milky Way. That's nearly 200 stars for every person living on Earth today!

Although we can't see all of it, astronomers have worked out how big the universe is and how many stars it has. There are about 100 billion billion stars, in around 100 billion galaxies. It's hard even to think about so many stars, let alone count them!

How hot is the Sun?

Like all stars, our Sun is a huge ball of super-hot gas. It is hottest in the middle – the temperature there is around 15 million °C.

The outside of the Sun is a lot cooler than the middle – only 6000 °C. But this is still 25 times hotter than the hottest kitchen oven!

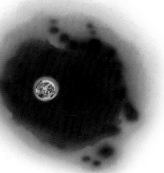

● Dark patches called sunspots come and go on the face of the Sun. They make it look as though it has chickenpox. Sunspots are dark because they are cooler and so give out less light than the rest of the Sun.

● Most sunspots are larger than the Earth.

● Plants and animals couldn't live without the Sun's heat and light.

● The Sun is the only star that's close enough to Earth for us to feel its heat. The next nearest star to Earth is called Proxima Centauri. Our Sun's light takes 8.3 minutes to reach us, but Proxima Centauri's takes 4.3 years!

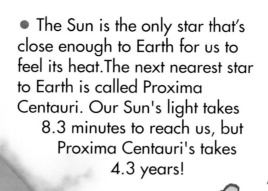

● The Sun uses more than 30 million truck loads of fuel every second!

Will the Sun ever go out?

One day the Sun will use up all its gas fuel and die. But this won't happen in your lifetime, or your children's, or even your great-great-great grandchildren's! Astronomers think that the Sun has enough gas fuel to last for at least another 5 billion years.

How many planets are there?

Our planet, the Earth, has eight neighbours. Together they make a family of nine planets which travel around the Sun. We call the Sun, and all the space bodies that whirl around it, the solar system.

Besides the Sun and the planets, the solar system includes moons, mini-planets called asteroids, and comets.

● Comets are rather like huge dirty snowballs. Most stay out on the edge of the solar system, but a few travel close to the Sun. These comets grow gas and dust tails, millions of kilometres long, when the Sun's heat starts to melt them.

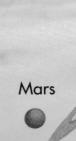

● The word planet comes from the Greek word *planetes*, which means wanderer.

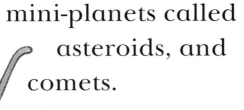

Mars

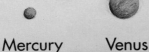

Mercury   Venus   Earth

Jupiter

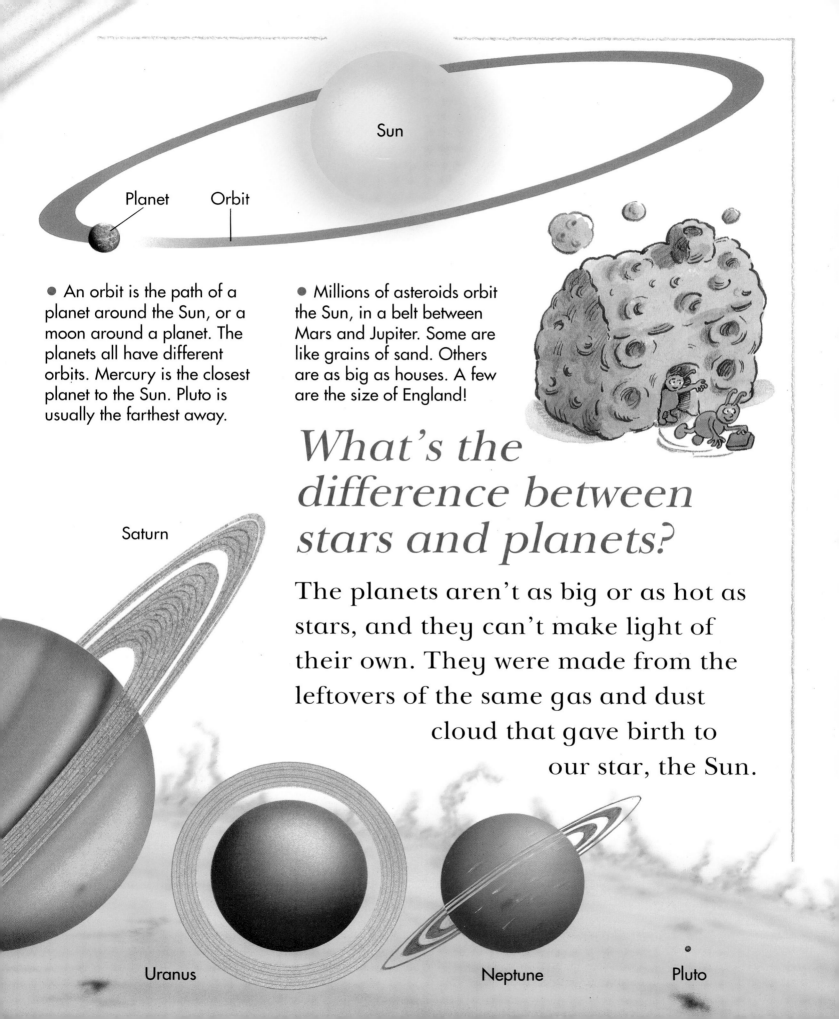

Sun

Planet   Orbit

- An orbit is the path of a planet around the Sun, or a moon around a planet. The planets all have different orbits. Mercury is the closest planet to the Sun. Pluto is usually the farthest away.

- Millions of asteroids orbit the Sun, in a belt between Mars and Jupiter. Some are like grains of sand. Others are as big as houses. A few are the size of England!

What's the difference between stars and planets?

The planets aren't as big or as hot as stars, and they can't make light of their own. They were made from the leftovers of the same gas and dust cloud that gave birth to our star, the Sun.

Saturn

Uranus

Neptune

Pluto

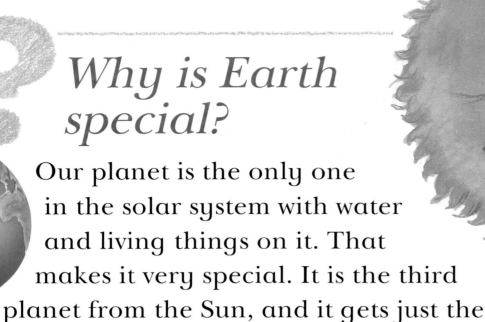

Why is Earth special?

Our planet is the only one in the solar system with water and living things on it. That makes it very special. It is the third planet from the Sun, and it gets just the right amount of heat and light to keep us alive. Any closer, and it would be too hot. Any farther away, and it would be too cold.

- When the Sun turns into a red giant star, it will swallow up Mercury and get so large that it will cover half of our midday sky.

- You can see what happens as the Earth spins if you turn a globe in the beam of light from a torch.

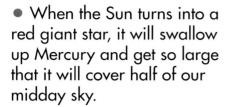

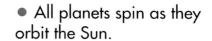

- All planets spin as they orbit the Sun.

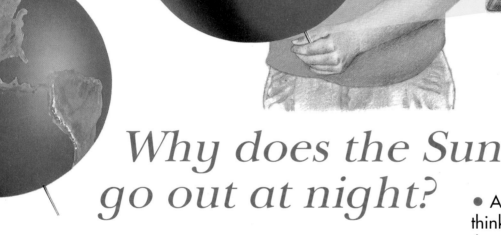

Why does the Sun go out at night?

- Although astronomers think that millions of stars in the universe have families of planets, no other solar systems have yet been found.

It gets dark at night because the Earth is spinning as it orbits the Sun. As parts of the Earth spin away from the Sun, they move out of its light into darkness. It takes a whole day and a night for the Earth to spin round once.

Which is the hottest planet?

Venus isn't the closest planet to the Sun, but it is the hottest. The temperature there can reach 500 °C – that's about eight times hotter than it gets in the Sahara Desert, the hottest place on Earth.

● Although Mercury (right) is closer to the Sun, Venus is hotter! This is because Venus is covered by clouds of gas which act like a blanket, keeping in the Sun's heat.

● Space probes have landed on Venus and sent back pictures and information to Earth. The probes were destroyed soon after landing, however, by the terrible climate on Venus.

- Mars is the next planet after ours from the Sun, and people once thought that like Earth it might have living things. Space probes were sent, but they didn't find any signs of life!

Which is the red planet?

- Mercury is covered in craters – hollows made by huge space rocks crashing into it.

- If you could visit Mercury, you would see that the Sun looks more than twice as big there as it does from Earth. This is because Mercury is so much closer to the Sun.

Mars is often called the red planet. The ground there is covered in dusty red soil, which gets swept up by the wind to make pink clouds! The rocks on Mars have lots of iron in them, and iron goes red when it rusts. A better name for Mars might be the rusty planet!

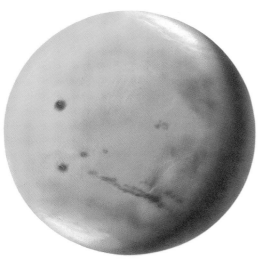

- Living things need water. If there is any on Mars, it is frozen inside its north and south polar ice caps.

The
Earth

Is the Earth round?

If you were an astronaut floating about in space, the Earth would look like a gigantic ball. It isn't perfectly round, though. Like a ball that's been gently squashed, it's slightly flatter at the top and bottom, and it bulges out just a little at the middle.

Equator

● The Earth measures 40,075 kilometres around its 'waist' – the equator. If you walked night and day, it would take you more than a year to get this far!

● The Earth looks blue from space. That's because nearly three-quarters of it is covered by the sea.

The crust is the rocky layer beneath your feet.

The mantle is a thick layer of rock. It's so hot that some of the rock has melted.

The core is made of metal. The outer core is runny and liquid, but the inner core is solid.

Outer core

Inner core

● It's very hot indeed at the centre of the Earth – more than 5000 °C. That's about 150 times hotter than a really scorching hot summer's day!

What is the Earth made of?

The Earth is made up of different layers of rock and metal. Some of the layers are hard, but others are so hot that they've melted and are runny – a bit like hot sticky toffee.

● The Earth's crust doesn't stop at the seashore. It goes on under the deepest oceans.

How old is the Earth?

Scientists think the Earth formed about 4,600 million years ago – although no one was there to see! They think the Moon formed then, too.

● Human beings are very new to the Earth. If you imagine our planet's 4600-million-year-long history squeezed into one year, people have only been around since late on 31 December!

▽ About 200 million years ago there was just one super-continent called Pangaea.

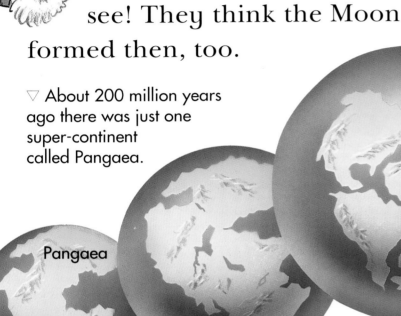

Pangaea

△ About 180 million years ago Pangaea began to break up.

● Continents are massive pieces of land. There are seven of them in all. Trace them from a map, and try to see how they once fitted together.

● Emus live in Australia, rheas in South America, and ostriches in Africa. They look similar, and none of them can fly. They may have been related to one kind of bird. It could have walked to all three continents millions of years ago, when the land was joined.

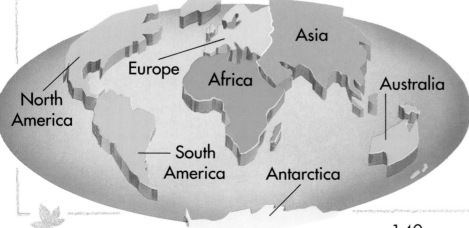

Asia

Europe

Africa

Australia

North America

South America

Antarctica

Has the Earth changed much?

Yes, it has! About 300 million years ago, most of the land was joined together in one big piece. Then it began to break up into smaller pieces called continents. These slowly drifted apart, until they reached the places they're in today.

▽ About 65 million years ago the continents drifted farther apart.

▽ Today, the continents are still drifting.

● North America and Europe are still moving apart by about 4 centimetres each year. That's about the length of your thumb.

How high is the sky?

The sky is part of an invisible skin of air around the Earth. This skin is called the atmosphere, and it reaches out into space for about 500 kilometres.

There's a very important gas called oxygen in the atmosphere – we all need to breathe oxygen to stay alive.

● The Earth is the only planet known to have enough oxygen for living things.

● If the Earth gets too hot, the ice at the Poles could melt. The seas would rise and drown many towns along the coasts.

What is the greenhouse effect?

The greenhouse effect is the name scientists have given to a hot problem. Waste gases from factories, power stations and cars are building up in the atmosphere and trapping too much heat close to the Earth. Our planet is slowly getting warmer – like a greenhouse in summer.

OZONE LAYER

3 Above the planes is the ozone layer. This works a bit like a sunblock, protecting us from the Sun's burning rays.

2 Planes fly in the next layer, high above the clouds where the skies are clear. The air is thinner here, and has less oxygen in it.

1 The atmosphere is made up of different layers. In the lowest layer, the air carries clouds and weather around the Earth.

What are clouds made of?

Some clouds look like they're made of cotton wool – but they're not! Clouds are made of billions of water droplets and ice crystals. These are so tiny and light that they float in the air.

● You'd need your umbrella on Mount Wai-'ale-'ale in Hawaii. It rains there for 350 days each year.

● Without rain, no plants would grow. Then what would we all eat?

When does rain fall from clouds?

Rain falls when water droplets in a cloud start joining together. They get bigger and heavier until, in the end, they are too heavy to float, and fall to the ground as rain.

● Have you ever heard of showers of frogs or fish? Well, they do happen. The animals are sometimes sucked up from ponds by extra-strong winds. Later on, they fall to the ground with the rain.

How cold is snow?

Snowflakes are water droplets that have frozen into crystals of ice. To stay frozen, they have to be at freezing point – that's 0 °C. If they get any warmer than this, snowflakes melt and fall to the ground as rain.

● The biggest snowman ever built was more than 22 metres high. That's about as tall as a seven-storey building.

Where do rivers begin?

● On some mountains, huge rivers of ice grind slowly downhill. These ice rivers are called glaciers.

Rivers start as tiny streams. Some streams begin where springs bubble out of the ground. Others form on mountains, when the tips of icy glaciers begin to melt. And some trickle out of lakes.

1 Rain falls on the hills and sinks into the ground.

2 Water trickles up out of a spring.

3 The stream joins others, and becomes a fast-flowing river.

4 The river reaches flatter land. It gets wider and flows more slowly.

Why do old rivers flow so slowly?

At the bottom of a hill, the ground becomes flatter, slowing the river down. Instead of rushing downhill in a straight line, the river flows in big bends called meanders.

146

Where do rivers end?

Most rivers end their journey at the sea. The mouth of the river is where fresh river water mixes with the salty water of the sea.

● The longest river in the world is the Nile River in Egypt. It flows for 6,670 kilometres.

● Some rivers don't flow into the sea. They flow into lakes instead, or drain into the ground.

● The world's shortest river is the D River in the USA. At just 37 metres, it is only as long as about ten canoes.

5 A river sometimes cuts through one of its bends – leaving behind a curvy ox-bow lake.

● Birds love feeding at a river mouth. They pull out the worms that live in the gooey mud!

6 At its mouth, the river joins the salty water of the sea.

How big is the ocean?

The ocean is truly ENORMOUS! It covers more than twice as much of the Earth as land does. In fact, it's made up of four oceans – the Pacific, the Atlantic, the Indian and the Arctic. Although these all have different names, they flow into each other to make one huge world ocean.

● Don't go for a swim in the Arctic Ocean. It's the coldest of the oceans, and for most of the year it's covered in ice.

Which is the biggest ocean?

● These drops of water show the oceans in order of size.

The Pacific is by far the biggest ocean in the world. It's larger than the other three oceans put together, and it's also much deeper. If you look at a globe, you'll see that the Pacific reaches halfway around the world.

What's the difference between a sea and an ocean?

People often use the words sea and ocean to mean the same thing. That's fine, but to a scientist, seas are just part of an ocean – the parts that are nearest to land. The Mediterranean Sea is between Africa and Europe, for example.

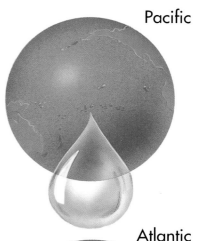

Pacific

Atlantic

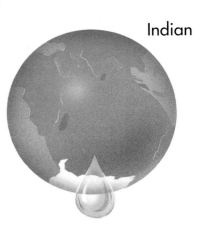

Indian

Arctic

149

Where do angels, clowns and parrots live?

Angelfish, clownfish and parrotfish are just some of the thousands of beautiful animals that live on coral reefs. Tropical fish like these often have dazzling colours and bold patterns.

● Coral reefs grow in shallow water in the warmest parts of the world.

Angelfish

Parrotfish

Imperial angelfish

● Giant clams live on coral reefs. Their shells are big enough to have a bath in!

What is a coral reef?

A coral reef is like a beautiful underwater hedge. It looks stony and dead – but it is really alive! Coral is made up of millions of tiny animals, which leave their hard skeletons behind when they die. Each new layer piles on to the old, slowly building the coral rock.

● Corals comes in all sorts of shapes – antlers, plates, mushrooms, feathers, daisies and even brains!

Where is the biggest reef?

The world's biggest coral reef lies in warm shallow seas off the northeast coast of Australia. It's called the Great Barrier Reef, and it stretches for more than 2,000 kilometres. It's so huge that it can be seen by astronauts up in space.

Clown fish

How often does it rain in a rainforest?

It rains almost every day in a rainforest, but it doesn't pour all day long. The air gets hotter and hotter, and stickier and stickier, until there's a heavy thunderstorm in the afternoon. After that, it's dry again.

● The world's biggest rainforest is in South America. It stretches for thousands of kilometres along the banks of the Amazon River.

Where are rainforests?

The places where rainforests grow are shown above in green. These are the world's warmest areas, near the equator.

● Anacondas are enormous snakes. They hide in the muddy waters of the Amazon, waiting for a tasty meal to pass by.

- Rainforests are home to over half of all the animals and plants that live on Earth.

- This book started life as a tree trunk! Most paper comes from coniferous trees, such as spruce and pine.

Where is the biggest forest?

The world's biggest forest stretches right the way across the top of Europe and Asia. The trees in this forest are conifers – they have hard narrow leaves called needles.

- Brown bears and wolves live in the dark forests of the North. Reindeer shelter there during the long cold winters.

What's it like at the Poles?

• Polar bears live at the North Pole, and penguins live at the South Pole. They never get the chance to meet!

The North and South Poles are at the very ends of the Earth. They are freezing cold places with biting winds. Ice and snow stretch as far as the eye can see – not the best place for a holiday!

• Antarctica is a huge ice-covered continent around the South Pole. In places, the ice is nearly 5 kilometres thick.

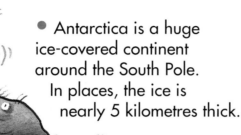

Which is the coldest place in the world?

Vostok Station is a really chilly spot in Antarctica. The temperature here is usually about -58 °C, but it has dropped to -89 °C – the coldest ever known!

• Mount Erebus must be the warmest spot in Antarctica. It's an active volcano!

Where do polar bears live?

Polar bears live around the Arctic Ocean, near the North Pole. Funnily enough, they've never lived in Antarctica, though there's plenty of food and just as much snow and ice there.

● Icebergs float in the sea. They were once part of rivers of ice called glaciers.

● Polar bears never slip on the ice. The rough skin and hair on the soles of their feet give them a bit of extra grip.

What is a desert?

Deserts are the driest parts of the world – places where it hardly ever rains. Most have less than 25 cm of rain a year – a tenth of the rain that falls every year in rainforests, the wettest parts of the world.

● Deserts aren't just the world's driest places. They're also the windiest.

Are all deserts hot?

In many of the world's deserts, it is hot enough in the daytime to fry an egg on a rock. Not all deserts are like this, though. Some deserts have baking hot summers and freezing cold winters, while others are chilly all year round.

● Even if you're heading for a hot desert, remember to pack a jumper. Although the daytime temperature can soar to over 40°C, it can drop to below 0°C at night. Brrrrrr!

- When it does rain in a desert, it can bucket down. All of a desert's annual rain may fall in one tremendous storm over two or three days.

- Even a sandy desert may be dotted with big rocks here and there. This huge boulder casts welcome shade during the hottest part of the day – time for people to shelter from the Sun's frizzling heat.

Are all deserts sandy?

No – some are gravelly, while others are rocky or even snowy. Antarctica is a cold snowy desert, for example, where there is no rain and little sun.

- Some deserts are a crazy paving pattern of dried-up salt flats – with a surface that's as hard as concrete.

Where is the world's biggest desert?

The largest desert in the whole world is the Sahara in North Africa. It's larger than Australia, and nearly the size of the entire USA.

Key to map

- **The driest deserts, where it hardly ever rains**

- **Deserts that have enough rain for some plants to grow**

- **Semi-deserts, with enough rain for shrubby plants to grow**

● At 86 m below sea level, the Death Valley desert is the lowest place in the USA.

● South America's Atacama Desert is the world's driest place. Parts of the Atacama had no rain at all between 1570 and 1971 – that's 401 years!

● About one fifth of all the land on Earth is desert.

NORTH AMERICA

Great Basin

Mojave

Sonoran

Chihuahuan

Equator

ATLANTIC OCEAN

SOUTH AMERICA

Sechura

Atacama

Patagonian

FOR SALE

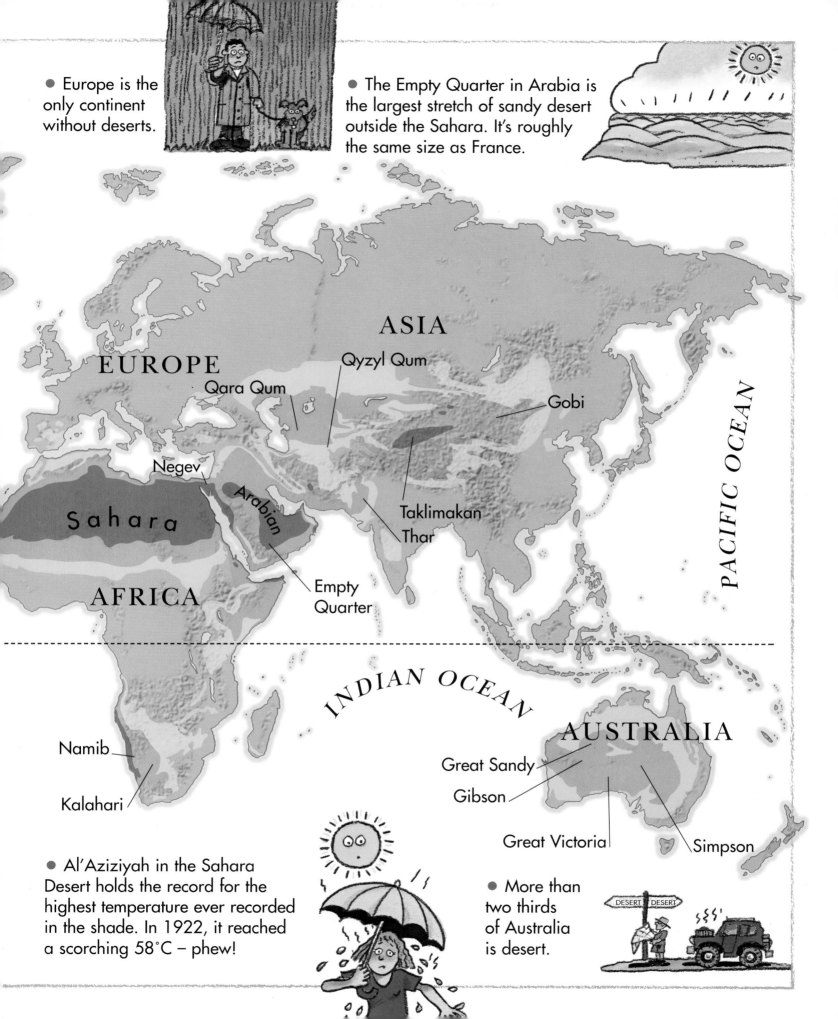

● Europe is the only continent without deserts.

● The Empty Quarter in Arabia is the largest stretch of sandy desert outside the Sahara. It's roughly the same size as France.

ASIA

EUROPE

Qyzyl Qum

Qara Qum

Gobi

Negev

Arabian

Taklimakan

Thar

Sahara

PACIFIC OCEAN

AFRICA

Empty Quarter

INDIAN OCEAN

Namib

AUSTRALIA

Great Sandy

Gibson

Kalahari

Great Victoria

Simpson

● Al'Aziziyah in the Sahara Desert holds the record for the highest temperature ever recorded in the shade. In 1922, it reached a scorching 58°C – phew!

● More than two thirds of Australia is desert.

DESERT DESERT

What is an oasis?

Although little water falls as rain in a desert, there are places where it rises to the surface from deep below the ground. If there's enough water all year round for plants to grow, we call that place an oasis.

● A qanat is a deep underground tunnel carved out by people to bring water into the desert.

When is there water in a wadi?

A wadi is a desert river valley, and most of the time it's as dry as a bone. When there's a rainstorm, however, the wadi fills quickly, and for a while it becomes a roaring, raging torrent of water.

● Every year in the Australian desert town of Alice Springs, people race up the dry bed of the Todd River carrying bottomless boats!

How does sunlight trick desert travellers?

There's nothing a thirsty desert traveller wants to see more than water. But sometimes the shimmering blue pool up ahead isn't water at all – it's just an image of the sky. These tricks of the light are called mirages.

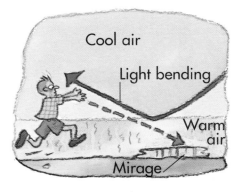

● A mirage happens when sunlight is 'bent' as it travels through hot air near the ground. The scientific name for this 'bending' is refraction.

What's the difference between a mountain and a hill?

Mountains are larger than hills, and mountainsides are often steep and tough to climb – unlike a hill's gentle slopes. Some experts say that if a peak is more than 600 metres higher than the surrounding land, then it is a mountain. Any less and it is a hill.

● A molehill is a tiny pile of soil which, like a mountain, rises steeply above the surrounding land.

● About a quarter of all land on Earth is mountainous.

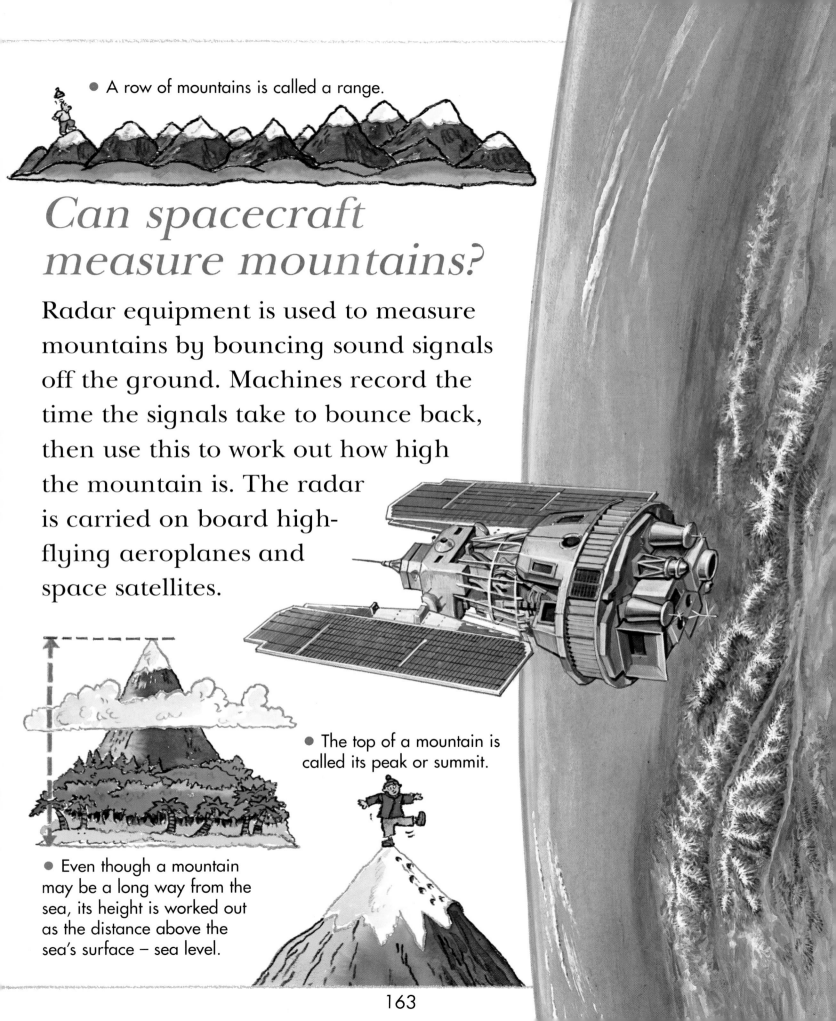

- A row of mountains is called a range.

Can spacecraft measure mountains?

Radar equipment is used to measure mountains by bouncing sound signals off the ground. Machines record the time the signals take to bounce back, then use this to work out how high the mountain is. The radar is carried on board high-flying aeroplanes and space satellites.

- The top of a mountain is called its peak or summit.

- Even though a mountain may be a long way from the sea, its height is worked out as the distance above the sea's surface – sea level.

163

Where is the world's highest mountain?

The highest place in the whole world is at the top of Mount Everest. This vast mountain is in the Himalayan ranges of central Asia, and it rises to 8,848 metres above sea level.

- Although only 4,205 metres of Mauna Kea stick up above sea level, this Hawaiian mountain is even taller than Everest. From its base on the ocean floor to its peak, Mauna Kea is an amazing 10,203 metres.

- The world's longest mountain range on land is the Andes, in South America, at about 7,200 kilometres long.

NORTH AMERICA

Alaska Range

Rocky Mountains

Appalachians

Sierra Nevada

ATLANTIC OCEAN

SOUTH AMERICA

Andes

Famous mountains

1 McKinley
6,194 m

2 Logan
5,951 m

3 Whitney
4,418 m

4 Popocatépetl
5,452 m

5 Cotopaxi
5,897 m

6 Aconcagua
6,959 m

7 Kilimanjaro
5,895 m

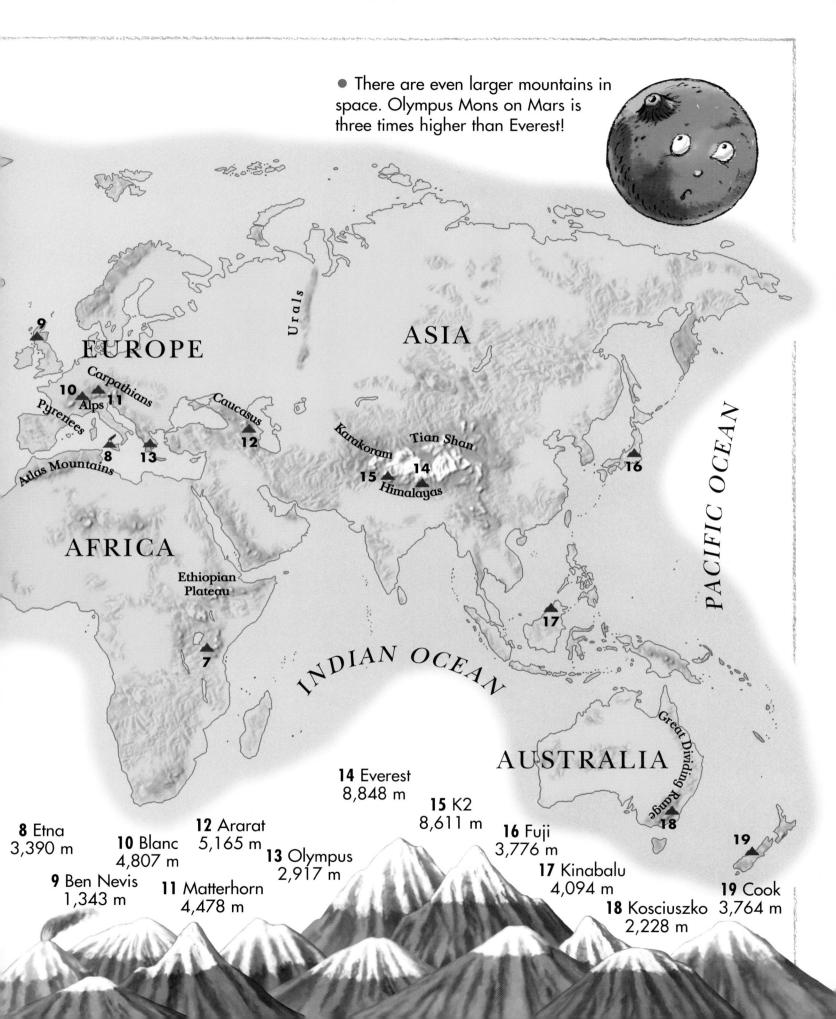

● There are even larger mountains in space. Olympus Mons on Mars is three times higher than Everest!

Urals

ASIA

EUROPE

Carpathians

10 Alps 11

Pyrenees

Caucasus

12

Atlas Mountains

8

13

Karakoram

Tian Shan

15 14

Himalayas

16

AFRICA

Ethiopian
Plateau

7

PACIFIC OCEAN

INDIAN OCEAN

17

AUSTRALIA

Great Dividing Range

18

14 Everest
8,848 m

15 K2
8,611 m

8 Etna
3,390 m

12 Ararat
5,165 m

10 Blanc
4,807 m

13 Olympus
2,917 m

16 Fuji
3,776 m

17 Kinabalu
4,094 m

19

9 Ben Nevis
1,343 m

11 Matterhorn
4,478 m

19 Cook
3,764 m

18 Kosciuszko
2,228 m

Which mountains grow into islands?

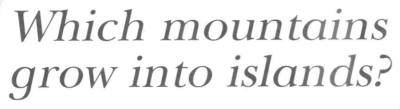

There are thousands of tiny islands dotted through the world's oceans, and most of them were made by volcanoes slowly growing up from the ocean floor.

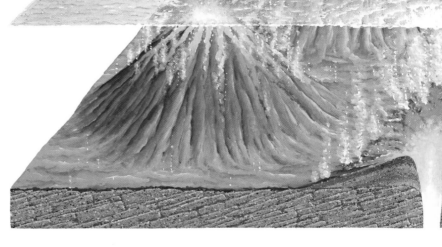

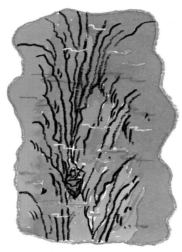

● With its bottom 11,033 metres below sea level, the world's deepest valley is the Mariana Trench in the Pacific Ocean.

● The world's longest mountain range is nearly all under water. It's called the Mid-Atlantic Ridge and it stretches for about 16,000 kilometres, from Iceland almost to Antarctica.

Mid-Atlantic Ridge

NORTH AMERICA

EUROPE

AFRICA

SOUTH AMERICA

ATLANTIC OCEAN

Can mountains sink?

Yes – an atoll is a ring-shaped island which can form around the rim of a sunken volcano. The atoll is made from limestone, and the limestone is made by tiny sea creatures called coral polyps.

Lagoon

Coral atoll

● The water in the middle of a coral atoll is called a lagoon.

What are black smokers?

Black smokers are strange chimney stacks that build up on the ocean floor and belch out steamy black clouds of boiling hot water. All kinds of weird and wonderful animals live near them, including red-and-white worms as long as cars.

What is a cave?

A cave is a natural hollow or crack in the ground that's big enough for a large animal, such as a human, to pass inside. Sometimes a cave is a single, roomlike area called a chamber. In other places, several chambers are connected by passages. This is called a cave system.

Which is the biggest cave chamber?

The record-holder is the Sarawak Chamber in the Gunung Mulu National Park, in the Malaysian region of Sarawak, on the island of Borneo. It's a massive 700 metres long, 415 metres wide, and 80 metres high.

● With a depth of 1,710 metres, the Voronja (or Krubera) Cave in Georgia, east of the Black Sea, is the deepest cave to be explored so far.

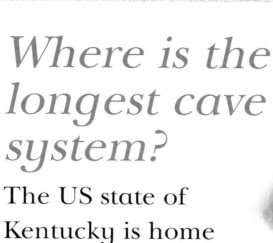

Where is the longest cave system?

The US state of
Kentucky is home
to the world's longest-
known cave system. It's
called Mammoth Cave, and
to date, explorers have mapped
about 570 kilometres of passages.
What's more, people think hundreds more
kilometres may be waiting to be discovered!

● There's enough
room inside the
Sarawak Chamber
to park 40 jumbo jets.

What are stalactites and stalagmites?

Stalactites and stalagmites are spectacular, stony structures that sometimes form inside limestone caves. Both are roughly carrot-shaped, but while stalactites hold tight to the cave roof, mighty stalagmites are mounted on the cave floor.

● Stalactites and stalagmites can sometimes join up to make a column. One of the world's tallest is in Spain's Nerja Cave. It measures around 32 metres from top to bottom.

Stalagmite

Stalactite

Why do stalactites hang down?

As acidic water seeps downwards, it dissolves the mineral calcite which makes up most of the limestone. When this liquid drips and dribbles from a cave roof, some of the water evaporates and changes into a gas, leaving some of the minerals behind, as solids. Over time, these minerals may grow downwards to build stalactites.

● Stalactites never get to be as large as stalagmites. That's because when a stalactite gets very big, it becomes too heavy and crashes down from the cave roof.

Do you get fried eggs in caves?

You certainly do. Stalactites and stalagmites aren't the only amazing sights to be found in caves. Minerals can form all kinds of other weird and wonderful shapes and come in every shade of the rainbow. In the Luray Caverns, in the US state of Virginia, there are two mineral formations that look just like fried eggs!

Column

● Flowstone looks like a stone waterfall.

● Cave pearls can be the size of ping-pong balls.

Flowstone

Cave pearls

● Soda straws are hollow and look like the straws you sip drinks through. They are the beginning of a stalactite.

How do caves form inside icy glaciers?

A glacier is a huge, thick mass of ice that builds up in freezing cold places like the poles. But even in the world's chilliest spots, the weather usually heats up a little in summer. These warmer temperatures can make some of the ice inside a glacier melt and begin to flow away through cracks. In its turn, the warmer, flowing water can melt more and more ice, until it carves out a glacial cave.

● If a glacial cave isn't too deep below the surface, sunlight can filter down through the ice to fill the cave with an eerie blue glow.

● Some of the most stunning glacier caves are in Iceland, the land of ice and fire. Heat from volcanoes at the glaciers' lowest edges melts the ice, creating caves inside the glaciers.

Where is the 'World of the Ice Giants'?

You'll have to take a trip to Austria to visit the 'World of the Ice Giants', or *Eisriesenwelt,* the world's biggest system of ice caves. Unlike glacial caves, ice caves form inside solid rock, as a cave's rock walls become coated in ice that stays frozen all year round.

● In parts of the 'World of the Ice Giants', the ice is 20 metres thick.

What is a lava tube?

It is a cave formed by lava, the hot, runny rock that pours out when a volcano blows its top! Sometimes, when lava flows downhill, its outer layers cool and harden into a solid crust, but its inner layers stay runny. If this runny lava drains away, a tube-like cave is left behind.

How does the sea scoop out caves?

Sea caves form along rocky coastlines, as waves pound grit and pebbles against the land, and make holes in the cliffs. Sea caves are often well hidden, with tiny entrances that are difficult to find and even harder to get to. It's one reason why smugglers used to stash their booty inside them.

What is a blowhole?

Sometimes, wave power can bash a hole in a sea cave's roof. This is called a blowhole. When the seawater rises at high tide, waves pounding into the cave are squeezed upwards to squirt out of the blowhole like a huge fountain.

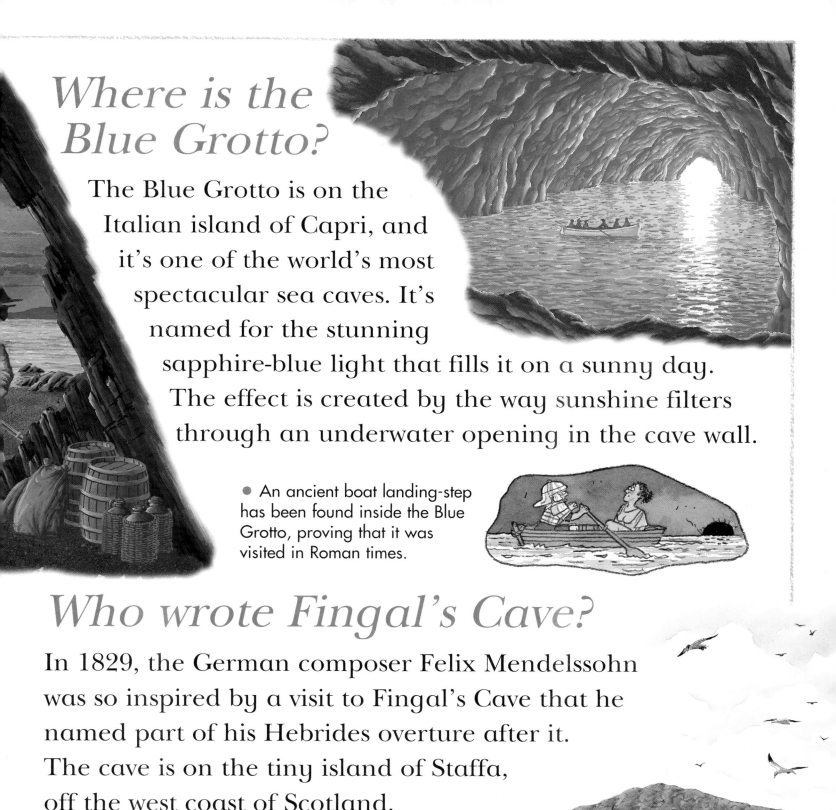

Where is the Blue Grotto?

The Blue Grotto is on the Italian island of Capri, and it's one of the world's most spectacular sea caves. It's named for the stunning sapphire-blue light that fills it on a sunny day. The effect is created by the way sunshine filters through an underwater opening in the cave wall.

● An ancient boat landing-step has been found inside the Blue Grotto, proving that it was visited in Roman times.

Who wrote Fingal's Cave?

In 1829, the German composer Felix Mendelssohn was so inspired by a visit to Fingal's Cave that he named part of his Hebrides overture after it. The cave is on the tiny island of Staffa, off the west coast of Scotland.

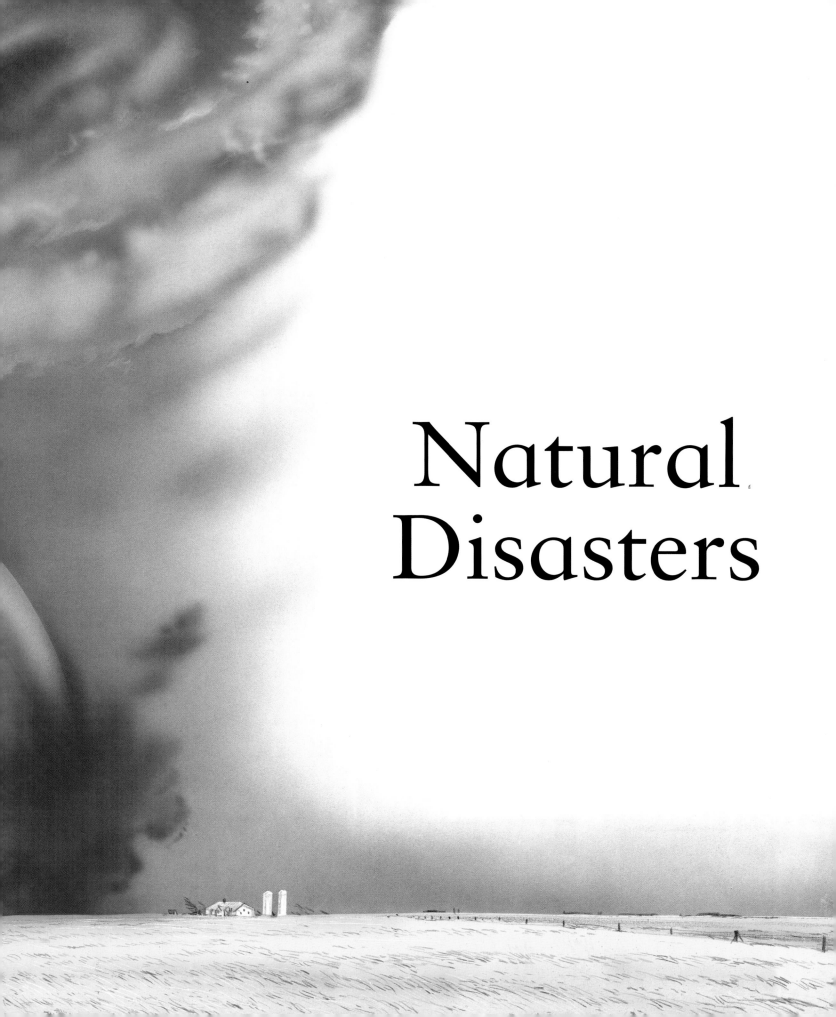

Natural
Disasters

Why do forests catch fire?

It doesn't take much to start a fire when plants are parched by a hot, rainless summer. A flash of lightning can sometimes spark a dry tree into flame, but most forest fires are caused by people being careless – for example by tossing away a match that is still alight. Fire can burn through a kilometre of forest in an hour, and if a fire rages out of control, it can devastate thousands of hectares of land.

● Indonesian forest fires raged for months in 1997, creating a choking blanket of smoke over much of Southeast Asia.

● Although forest fires can be damaging, some plants need their help to produce new seedlings. Banksias are Australian shrubs whose nutlike seed pods stay tightly shut until triggered open by the heat of a bush fire.

Who bombs fires?

In some countries, firefighters use a specially designed plane to combat fires. The plane can skim over the surface of a lake or the sea and scoop up thousands of litres of water into its tanks. Then the plane flies back to the fire to bomb the flames with its watery load.

● As many as 15,000 bush fires are reported in Australia each year.

How can you fight fire with fire?

A firebreak is a cleared strip of land ahead of a fire, where there's no fuel left to feed the flames. Firefighters sometimes set mini-fires of their own to help clear the ground.

When does a wind become a gale?

The faster the wind blows, the more powerful and dangerous it can be. The Beaufort scale measures wind speed as force 0 to 12 by its effect on the surrounding landscape. A gentle breeze is force 3, for instance – a 12 to 19 km/h wind that rustles twigs. A moderate gale is force 7 – a 50 to 61 km/h wind that makes whole trees sway!

● Force 10 is a whole gale – an 89 to 102 km/h wind that can uproot trees. Storms are force 11, and hurricanes are force 12.

● In March 1993, the eastern coast of Canada and the USA was struck by a savage blizzard carried on hurricane force winds. Thousands of buildings were destroyed or damaged, and the weather was so severe that it was named the Storm of the Century.

Why are blizzards dangerous?

Freezing cold winds can whip up the sudden blinding snowstorms we call blizzards. These can pile up huge snowdrifts, stopping traffic in its tracks and making it impossible for people to go to work or school!

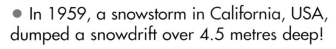

● In 1959, a snowstorm in California, USA, dumped a snowdrift over 4.5 metres deep!

Why did people shoot at clouds?

Hailstones can be the size of cricket balls and can cause enormous damage. In some countries, farmers used to try protecting their crops by firing big guns into clouds to stop the hail. Scientists are unsure if the guns really worked.

● In 1882, in Iowa, USA, two living frogs were found inside big hailstones! They were probably sucked up by a twister.

How much damage can a hurricane do?

With winds roaring at more than 117 km/h, hurricanes are the fiercest storms on earth. They start above warm tropical seas, and if a severe hurricane reaches land, it can flatten forests, smash houses, flip over cars, and even lift boats out of the water!

● Hurricanes can bring torrential rain and crashing waves, and sweep floods of seawater in over the coast. Once on land, the howling winds lose power and quickly die away.

Where is a hurricane's eye?

The eye of a hurricane is a central zone where the wind is fairly calm and there are no big storm clouds. The fast and furious hurricane winds move in a spiral around the eye.

● Each hurricane is given a name. The first of the year usually begins with A, such as Hurricane Alice. The second begins with B, and so on through the alphabet. Few names begin with the letters Q, U, X, Y or Z though!

What do hurricanes, typhoons and cyclones have in common?

They're all words for the same thing – and they all spell trouble! The word 'hurricane' is used in North and South America, 'typhoon' in the Far East, and 'cyclone' in Australia and India.

● Special weather planes help scientists to track hurricanes so they can issue warnings to people.

What wind can sink a ship?

Hurricanes are just as dangerous out at sea as they are on land. Most waves are caused by wind blowing across the water's surface, and a hurricane can whip up a 30-metre-high wall of water. When a freak wave this size smashes down, it can sink even large ships in minutes.

How do sailors know a storm is on its way?

Scientists use planes, ships and satellites to keep a watchful eye on the weather. Information is passed on to the rest of us via TV and radio stations, and sailors make sure they tune in for regular updates.

● Vicious gales and high tides can combine to cause devastating floods in low-lying coastal areas, endangering people and damaging their homes.

Which boats are unsinkable?

Lifeboats race to the rescue during shipwrecks. Modern lifeboats can cope with really wild weather – if a big wave tips one over, it flips back upright!

Why are twisters so dangerous?

'Twister' is a nickname for a tornado, a spinning windstorm that's usually born inside a huge thundercloud. The tornado snakes down to the ground, where it acts like a vacuum cleaner, sucking up everything in its path. Tornadoes are narrower than hurricanes, but they can be just as devastating.

● The world's worst place for tornadoes is Tornado Alley, a narrow belt of land that stretches across several US states.

What is a waterspout?

If a tornado forms over a lake or sea, it sucks up water and is called a waterspout. When its winds die down, it can drop its load of water like a bomb.

● If you're ever caught in a shower of fish, it's because a waterspout has sucked them up from a lake or the sea!

Where can you see a devil?

Hot air will sometimes swirl up from dry desert land, carrying dust and sand more than 150 metres high – this is a dust devil!

Where can wind strip paint off a car?

When a windstorm blows up in the desert, it blasts sand at anything in its path. Sand can strip the surface from all sorts of tough materials – even cars. That's why wood is smoothed with sandpaper and stone is polished with sandblasting machines!

● A sprinkling of sand from the Sahara Desert has been known to fall in Britain, thousands of kilometres away.

What is the Dust Bowl?

The Dust Bowl is a region in the USA's Midwest whose name dates back to the 1930s. There was so little rain in those years that the soil dried to dust and was blown away by windstorms. No crops grew, and farming families had to abandon their land and homes.

● Ancient rock paintings show that the Sahara was once far wetter and greener, and that giraffes and elephants grazed there.

How can a child be so destructive?

●La Niña has the opposite effect to El Niño. In Australia and Indonesia, for example, La Niña brings rain and good conditions for farming.

Warm and cold ocean currents help to shape the world's climate. In the Pacific Ocean, a cold current called La Niña (Spanish for 'the girl') usually flows west from South America to Indonesia. But every three to seven years, a warm current called El Niño ('the boy') flows eastwards in the opposite direction instead. Sometimes El Niño is strong, causing disastrous weather, including droughts, hurricanes and floods, from Alaska to Australia.

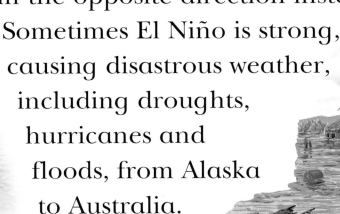

When does mud slide?

If torrentially heavy rain pelts down onto a steep mountain slope, it can turn loose soil into liquid mud and wash it away. Sometimes, a roaring river of mud sweeps down off the mountain, drowning everything in its path.

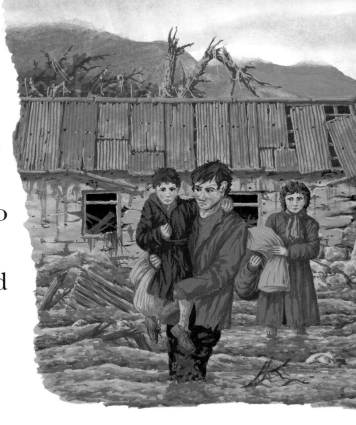

● The waters rose incredibly quickly when flash floods struck southern Mozambique in February 2000. There was so little time to escape that thousands of people were trapped for days on house roofs and in treetops.

What makes floods happen in a flash?

Flash floods got their name because they happen so quickly. Torrential rain can swamp a river or stream, making it suddenly burst its banks and spill out over the surrounding countryside.

• When a Colombian volcano blew its top in 1985, the heat melted its icecap and created mudflows called lahars which buried a whole town.

• Lahars can surge downhill at almost 100 km/h.

How do floods help?

When rivers burst their banks, they dump rich mud on the land which helps farmers to grow crops. The ancient Egyptians, for example, built their great civilization on the narrow strip of fertile farming land created by the River Nile flooding every year. The rest of their huge country was dry, dusty desert.

• Noah's Flood may have happened when the Mediterranean Sea broke through a strip of land, turning a freshwater lake into the salty Black Sea.

When does snow race at 300 km/h?

Snow can break away from a mountain slope and crash downhill at breakneck speed. This is an avalanche, and it can be triggered by anything from an earthquake to the swish of a skier's skis. The worst avalanches race along as fast as an express train, roaring louder than thousands of lions, as they bury homes and villages, railways and roads.

● Watch where you yodel in Switzerland – loud noises are another way of setting off an avalanche!

● During World War I, soldiers fired their guns to set avalanches off on their enemies.

Who is an avalanche victim's best friend?

No avalanche rescue team would be complete without its specially trained dogs. With their keen sense of smell, dogs are brilliant at sniffing out people hidden under the snow. And as soon as they find someone, the dogs start digging a rescue tunnel.

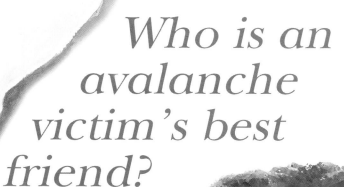

What makes land slide?

Disasters, such as avalanches and landslides, are most common in mountainous regions where there are no trees. Trees help keep land safe because they bury their roots down into the ground, anchoring it and stopping it from being swept away.

What happens in an earthquake?

A small earthquake makes the ground tremble. A powerful one makes it shudder and shake like a ship rocking on the ocean, and even crack wide open. The most devastating earthquakes can move mountains, make rivers change course, and bring entire cities tumbling down to the ground.

● In Japanese legend, earthquakes were triggered by a giant catfish called Namazu wriggling about.

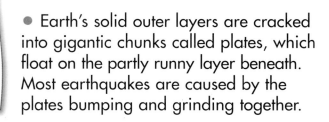

● Earth's solid outer layers are cracked into gigantic chunks called plates, which float on the partly runny layer beneath. Most earthquakes are caused by the plates bumping and grinding together.

When does soil turn into soup?

In areas with soft, wet soil, an earthquake can sometimes make the ground act like it's a liquid. Buildings sink, and stay firmly stuck even when the shaking stops and the ground becomes solid again.

● Laser beams are used to measure ground movement and help warn when an earthquake is coming.

How do we measure earthquakes?

An instrument called a seismometer is used to measure the vibrations, or shaking movements, of the ground in an earthquake. In some seismometers, a pen records the vibrations on paper wrapped around a turning drum. The pen is fixed to a weight and stays still during the quake, while the drum bounces about.

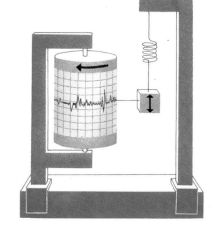

Which mountains spit fire?

If you ever see huge fiery clouds spurting out of a mountain, you can be sure it's a volcano – and what's worse, it's blowing its top! The most violent volcanoes explode like bombs, spitting out clouds of hot ash, chunks of solid rock, and fountains of the runny rock we call lava.

Why do volcanoes blow their tops?

Deep beneath a violent volcano is a vast chamber. Hot runny rock and gases build up here until they blast upwards under immense pressure through cracks in the earth's crust.

● Scientists who study volcanoes are called vulcanologists, after Vulcan, the Roman god of fire.

196

Where can you see rivers of rock?

Sometimes a red-hot river of lava pours out of a volcano and flows down its sides. The runny rock can reach temperatures of over 1,000°C – much, much hotter than an oven – and flow faster than you can run!

● As if volcanoes weren't dangerous enough, their ash clouds can become electrically charged and produce lightning!

What is an avalanche of ash?

Volcanic ash can be even more dangerous than lava. Sometimes ash clouds are not thrown up into the air, but roll down over the sides of a volcano like an avalanche. As they race downhill, these scorching-hot ash clouds burn, boil or melt everything in their path.

● Violent volcanoes can affect earth's climate, by throwing up ash clouds that shut out the sun's light. The eruption of Indonesia's Mount Tambora in 1815, for example, was followed by worldwide bad weather.

● When Mount Pinatubo in the Philippines erupted in 1991, an avalanche of ash destroyed land as far as 17 kilometres away.

Which volcano buried a Roman town?

When Italy's Mount Vesuvius erupted in August CE79, ash fell like snow over the Roman town of Pompeii, burying it in 6-metre-deep drifts. Then it rained. Afterwards the ash set like concrete, freezing the town in time until it was first excavated in the 1860s.

● Despite its chilly name, Iceland is a real hot spot with hundreds of volcanoes – lava has even set houses on fire!

How can volcanoes be good for you?

Although volcanic ash can be so destructive, it brings benefits as well. As the ash weathers down, it enriches the soil and helps farmers to grow bumper harvests.

How big can waves get?

When an average tsunami wave reaches the shore, it rears up into a 20-metre-high monster. But the tallest in modern times was 85 metres high – almost as high as the Statue of Liberty in New York City Harbor!

● Tsunamis can speed across the ocean at 1,000 km/h – as fast as a jet plane!

● A tsunami may have played a major role in the mysteriously sudden end of the Minoan civilization on the Greek island of Crete around 3,500 years ago. Gigantic 40-metre-high waves are thought to have smashed into Crete at that time, wiping out coastal towns and the entire Minoan fleet.

What sets off tsunamis?

Unlike ordinary ocean waves, which are mainly whipped up by the wind blowing over the water's surface, most tsunamis are shocked into life on the ocean floor. Underwater earthquakes, landslides and volcanic eruptions are all violent enough to kick-start a tsunami.

● When a volcano blew the Indonesian island of Krakatau apart in 1883, so much rock was hurled into the sea that tsunami waves were set off. The monster waves even picked up a ship and dumped it in the jungle on the nearby island of Sumatra.

What is dangerous about space rocks?

Earth is under constant attack from space rocks. Most are no bigger than a pebble and burn up as they plunge through the air. But every now and then, a big rock smashes into the ground and blasts out a hole called a crater.

● Space rocks that hit the ground are called meteorites.

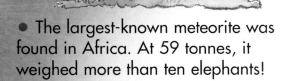

● The largest-known meteorite was found in Africa. At 59 tonnes, it weighed more than ten elephants!

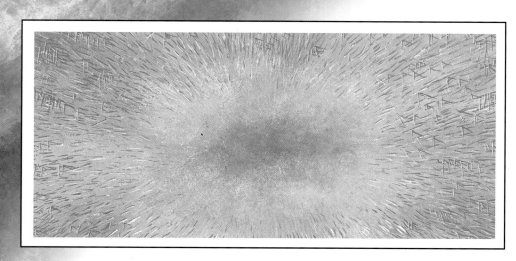

When a huge space rock exploded high above Siberia in 1908, it flattened a city-sized area of forest on the ground below.

Which was the greatest disaster on earth?

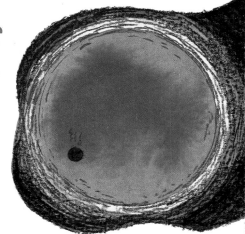

Many scientists think a massive meteorite strike killed off the dinosaurs 65 million years ago. The blast blew up enough dust to block out the sun's rays for months. Without sunlight, plants died. Cold and hunger killed off the plant-eating dinosaurs first, and then the meat-eaters.

One day the sun will swell into a red giant star and boil away earth's life-giving water. Don't worry, though, this won't happen for another 5 billion years.

Where do thunderstorms start?

Thunderstorms start in the huge black thunderclouds that sometimes gather at the end of a hot summer's day. Inside the clouds, strong winds hurl the water droplets around, and the cloud crackles with electricity. It flashes through the sky in great dazzling sparks, which we call lightning.

● It's safest to stay inside during a thunderstorm. Never shelter under a tree – it might get struck by lightning.

● An American man was struck by lightning seven times! Roy C. Sullivan had his hair set alight twice and his eyebrows burnt off. He even lost a big toenail.

● Lightning can travel as far as 140,000 kilometres in 1 second flat!

- To find out how far away a storm is, count the number of seconds between the lightning and the thunder. The storm is 1 kilometre away for every 3 seconds you count.

- The biggest thunderclouds tower 16 kilometres into the air. That's nearly twice the height of Mount Everest.

What is thunder?

Sparks of lightning are incredibly hot. As they flash through the sky, they heat the air so quickly that it makes a loud booming noise like an explosion. This is thunder.

Where does forked lightning come from?

A blinding river of light zigzags through the sky. This is lightning, a giant electrical spark that begins inside towering thunderclouds. Lightning heats the air in its path until it is very hot – hotter than the sun's surface – and the air explodes in a deafening crash of thunder!

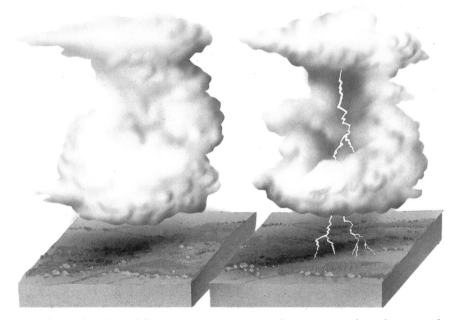

● A thundercloud becomes electrically charged when strong winds toss water droplets, ice crystals and hailstones up and down inside it.

● As the water droplets and ice crystals jostle about, they generate a huge charge of static electricity. This charge is released in brilliant flashes of lightning.

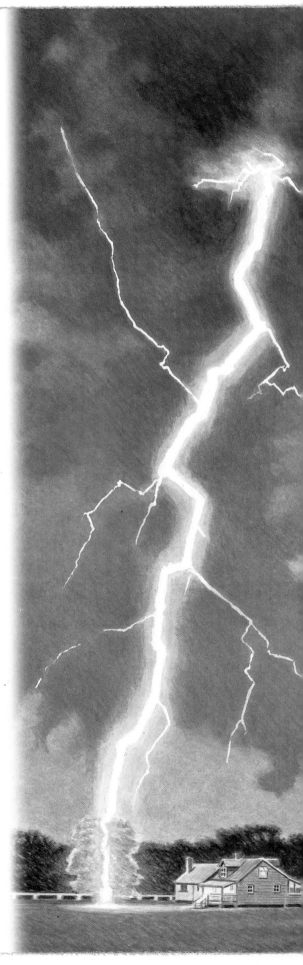

● The Vikings believed that lighting was made by the god Thor hurling his hammer, and that thunder was the rumble of his chariot's wheels.

What is ball lightning?

Eerie, glowing balls of light are sometimes seen during thunderstorms, floating a little way above the ground. This spooky effect is called ball lightning. Scientists are not sure what causes it, but the balls may be glowing hot gases given off when forked lightning strikes the ground.

● If lightning hits sandy ground, the heat can melt the sand. As it cools into a solid again, it forms a glassy sculpture of the lightning flash's path.

● Lightning once struck the Empire State Building in New York, USA, 15 times in 15 minutes!

Animal Kingdom

What's the difference between sharks and dolphins?

Although sharks and dolphins look alike, they belong to two very different animal groups. Sharks are a kind of fish, but dolphins are members of another group, the mammals.

• You don't look anything like a dolphin, but you are a mammal, too!

• If an animal breathes air through lungs, and its babies feed on their mother's milk, it's a mammal. Most mammals have some fur or hair on their bodies.

Lungs

- If an animal has feathers and hatches out of a hard-shelled egg, it's a bird. All birds have wings, and most of them can fly.

- If an animal has six legs and three parts to its body, it's an insect. There are more kinds of insect in the world than all the other kinds of animal put together.

Abdomen

Head

Thorax

- If an animal has damp slimy skin, and is born in water but lives much of its life on land, it's an amphibian. Baby amphibians hatch out of jelly-like eggs.

- If an animal has a dry scaly skin and is born on land, it's a reptile. Most reptiles lay eggs with leathery skins.

Scaly skin

Fin

- If an animal lives in water, breathing through gills and using fins to move, it's a fish. Most fish lay jelly-like eggs which hatch into baby fish.

Gills

● Female Queen Alexandra's birdwings are the world's biggest butterflies. Their wings are almost as big as this page!

● The blue whale is so long that eight elephants could stand along its back.

Giraffe
5.5 metres tall

Elephant
3.5 metres tall
7 tonnes

Ostrich
2.5 metres tall

● The giraffe is the tallest land animal. With its long neck, it can reach as high as a two-storey house.

● The mighty African elephant is almost three times as tall as you are. It can weigh as much as seven cars.

● The ostrich is the world's tallest and heaviest bird. It's as tall as a single-decker bus!

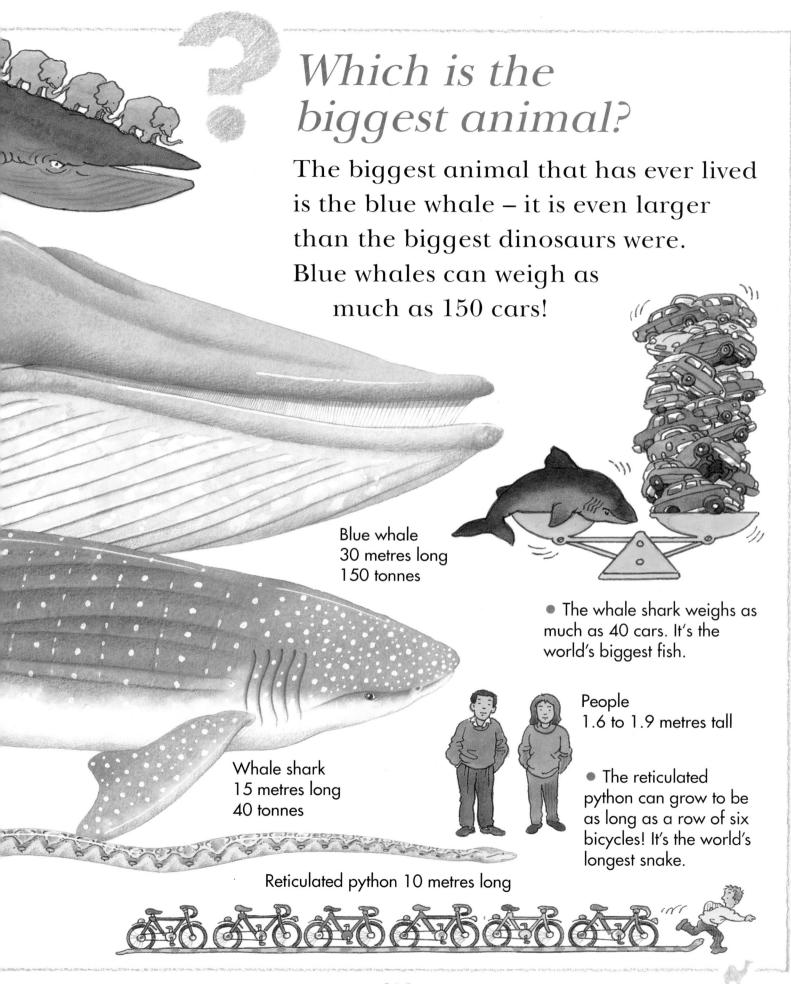

Which is the biggest animal?

The biggest animal that has ever lived is the blue whale – it is even larger than the biggest dinosaurs were. Blue whales can weigh as much as 150 cars!

Blue whale
30 metres long
150 tonnes

● The whale shark weighs as much as 40 cars. It's the world's biggest fish.

People
1.6 to 1.9 metres tall

Whale shark
15 metres long
40 tonnes

● The reticulated python can grow to be as long as a row of six bicycles! It's the world's longest snake.

Reticulated python 10 metres long

What are a horse's good points?

When people talk about a horse's points, they mean the different parts of its body, such as its muzzle or its tail. The overall shape and arrangement of a horse's whole body is called its conformation.

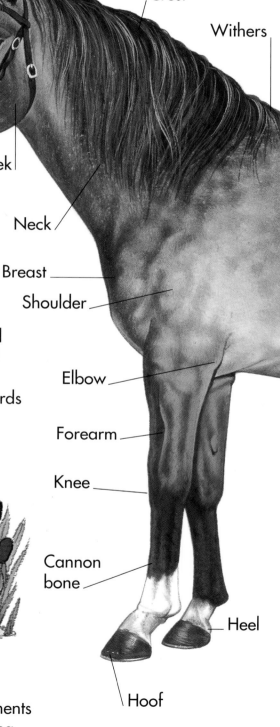

Forelock
Poll
Mane
Crest
Withers
Cheek
Nostril
Muzzle
Neck
Breast
Shoulder
Elbow
Forearm
Knee
Cannon bone
Heel
Hoof

• A female horse is called a mare, while a male horse is called a stallion.

• The ancient Greek word for horse was *hippos*, and our word hippopotamus comes from two Greek words meaning 'river horse'.

• Bows for musical instruments like the cello are often strung with hair from a horse's tail.

Do horses have hands?

Not in the same way that you do!
A horse's hands are the units used to
measure its height from the ground to
its withers – one hand equals about ten cm.

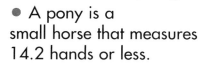

● A pony is a
small horse that measures
14.2 hands or less.

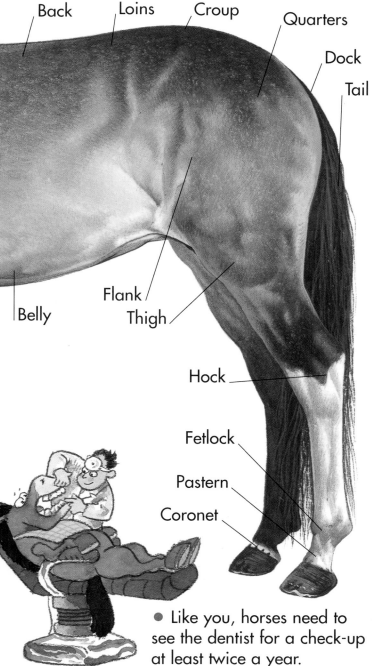

Back Loins Croup Quarters

Dock

Tail

Belly

Flank
Thigh

Hock

Fetlock

Pastern

Coronet

● Like you, horses need to
see the dentist for a check-up
at least twice a year.

How can you tell a horse's age?

Horses mainly eat grass, and
munching away at this sort of
tough plant food is very hard
on teeth. Experts can get a
good idea of a horse's age by
looking at the way its teeth are
wearing as it gets older.

How can you tell if a horse is happy?

Although horses can't talk like we do, you can tell how a horse is feeling from its body language. A happy horse will hold its head and its tail up high, for example.

● Zebras belong to the same animal family as horses, and so do donkeys and asses.

Alert

Angry

Afraid

● Even a well-trained animal can have its off days, so never walk or stand close to a horse's back legs – you might get kicked.

Content

Do horses like company?

They certainly do. Horses love hanging out in a herd – that's what we call a group of horses.

● Horses can sleep standing up. If they're in a herd, one horse will usually stay awake and watch out for danger while the others are dozing.

When is a horse a dam?

A mare is called a dam when she has babies. The babies are called foals, and a foal's father is its sire. Usually, a mother horse gives birth to one foal at a time, after carrying it inside her for about a year.

● Horses are sometimes bred with donkeys – a mule has a donkey sire and a horse dam, while a hinny has a horse sire and a donkey dam. However, mules and hinnies can't have babies of their own.

How many kinds of horse are there?

There are now more than 200 breeds of horse and pony. Members of a breed share certain characteristics, such as colour and height, and pass them on to their foals.

● A short white marking on a horse's leg is called a sock, while a longer one is a stocking!

Which are the smallest horses?

Ponies are, of course, and the world's tiniest breed is the Falabella. Small breeds are measured in centimetres, not hands, and Falabellas grow to only about 75 centimetres high.

● There are special names for the different colour combinations of a horse's coat, skin, mane and tail.

1. Chestnut
2. Appaloosa
3. Fleabitten grey
4. Palomino
5. Black
6. Dapple grey
7. Piebald
8. Bay
9. Dun
10. Brown
11. Strawberry roan

● Falabellas are too small to be ridden, but Shetland ponies grow a little taller and are favourites with young riders.

Which are the biggest horses?

The giants of the horse world are the group of breeds known as heavy horses. The giant of these heavy horse breeds is the Shire. Shire horses grow to around 17 hands high and can weigh as much as a tonne.

● The tallest-ever horse was a Shire born in 1846. By the time it was six, it measured 21.25 hands.

● The fringes of hair around a Shire's feet are called feathers.

Why do animals have skeletons inside their bodies?

Not all animals have skeletons, but most large ones do. This is because the bigger an animal is, the more it needs a strong sturdy framework to hold its body together and carry its weight. Skeletons also protect soft inside parts, like brains and hearts.

Backbone

● Animals without backbones are called invertebrates. Insects, spiders, snails, worms, jellyfish, prawns and crabs are all invertebrates.

● Animals with backbones are called vertebrates. Fish are vertebrates, and so are amphibians, reptiles, birds and mammals.

Backbone

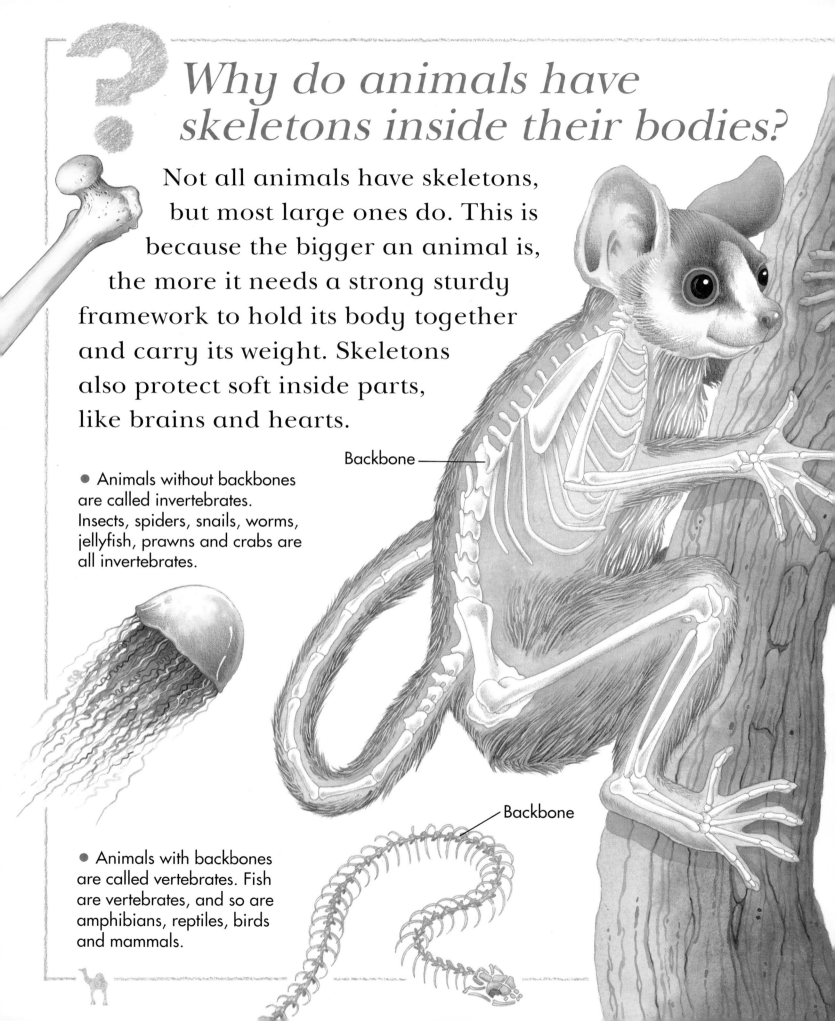

- Most animals' skeletons are made of bone, but a shark's skeleton is made of gristle. This isn't as hard as bone, but it's still tough. You have some at your nose tip.

Millipede

- Insects, spiders, scorpions, centipedes and millipedes all have tough exoskeletons.

- Lobsters, crabs and some beetles have really tough exoskeletons that work like armour, to protect them from attack.

- Squid are the biggest kind of invertebrate. The longest one ever found measured more than 17 metres from its head to the tip of its tentacles – longer than eight scuba divers!

Which animals have skeletons on the outside?

Most smaller animals have tough skins called exoskeletons. These outside skeletons do the same job as inside ones. They protect and support the animals' soft bodies.

- To grow larger, an animal has to break out of its old exoskeleton and grow a new one.

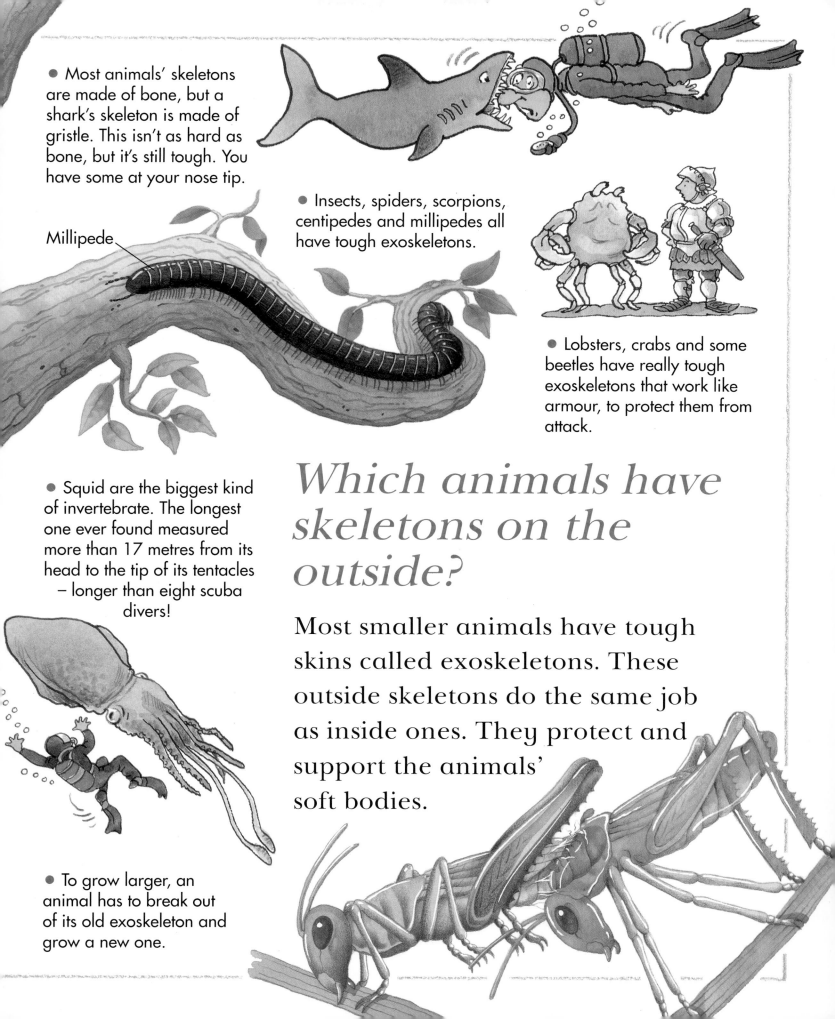

Why do pandas have one baby at a time?

A mother giant panda gives her cub so much love and attention that she can only cope with one at a time. By looking after her cub for a year or more, she is helping to make sure that her baby survives.

● There aren't many pandas left. Zookeepers fly their pandas around the world so they can meet other pandas – and hopefully have babies.

Which animals lay hundreds of eggs?

Most frogs and toads lay hundreds of eggs in a big frothy mass called spawn. Many of the eggs are eaten, but some of them survive and hatch into tadpoles.

● The giant clam may have the biggest family of all. Every year the female lays a great cloud of eggs – at least a billion of them!

Which family is always identical?

Each time a nine-banded armadillo gives birth, she has four identical babies. They are either all female or all male. This is because a single egg inside the mother splits into four, and all four parts begin to grow – into identical quadruplets!

● Albatross mums lay just one egg every two years. The chick is looked after by its parents for about ten months, until it's big enough to fly.

223

Why do camels have humps?

A camel's hump is its own built-in food cupboard. By living off the fat stored in its hump, a camel can go for as long as two weeks without eating. Camels need their humps because they live in deserts, where food and water are hard to find.

Why do elephants have trunks?

An elephant's trunk is a helpful tool. It can be used to pull down leaves and branches to eat. It also makes a good hose – elephants can squirt dust or water over themselves to keep cool.

● Elephants say 'hello' to friends by shaking trunks with them.

● An elephant's trunk is a bit like a hand. Using its tip, an elephant can pick up something as small as a button.

- Arabian camels have one hump.

- Bactrian camels have two humps.

- A thirsty camel can drink ten buckets of water in just 10 minutes!

Why do giraffes have long necks?

A giraffe's long neck makes it tall enough to eat the leaves at the top of trees. Other animals cannot reach as high, so the giraffe has lots to eat.

- A giraffe's tongue is half a metre long!

Which fish hunts with a hammer?

The hammerhead shark has a huge head shaped like a hammer. But this tool is for hunting, not banging in nails. The shark's eyes and nostrils are at each end of the hammer. As the shark swims, it swings its head from side to side, searching for a meal.

● The Portuguese man-of-war catches its tea in its long, stinging tentacles.

Which is the most shocking fish?

Some fish give off electric shocks to protect themselves or to stun animals they want to eat. The most shocking ocean fish is the torpedo ray. If you could switch it on, it would light up a light bulb!

● Thousands of mackerel swim together in one huge shoal. Their enemies find it difficult to pick out a single fish from the shimmering, silvery mass.

Which fish look like stones?

Stonefish look just like lumps of rock – but they're far more dangerous. If attacked, a stonefish uses the needle-sharp spines on its fins to stab its enemy with a deadly poison.

● The leafy sea dragon looks just like a ragged strand of seaweed. What a perfect disguise!

How do desert foxes keep their cool?

The kit fox's big ears work like radiators, giving off heat and cooling its body down. They also help it to listen out for enemies such as hyenas.

● The jack rabbit is another desert animal with big ears to help it keep cool.

Which animal has its own sun parasol?

Unlike most other small desert animals, ground squirrels spend their days out in the Sun. They shelter from the midday heat under their own sun parasols – their tails!

● Many ground squirrels also use their tails for signalling to each other if danger is near.

- The golden mole spends most of its life burrowing through the sand. It can tunnel more than 4 km in one night.

- Many desert animals have light-coloured fur, which helps keep them cool by reflecting sunlight.

- The elf owl shelters from the hot desert sunlight in a hole in a tall saguaro cactus.

Why do desert animals love the dark?

It's a lot cooler out of the Sun than in it, so many small desert animals shelter from the daytime heat in underground burrows. They come out to hunt for food at night, or in the early morning and evening.

Which baby has the best mother?

A baby gorilla has one of the best mums in the world. A grown-up gorilla may look a bit frightening to us, but she's loving and gentle to her young. As well as grooming the baby, she feeds it for up to three years, and protects and helps it for longer still.

● Gorillas are a type of ape – along with chimpanzees, gibbons and orang-utans. All the apes make jolly good mums.

Which baby has the worst mother?

The female European cuckoo can't be bothered to look after her chicks. This lazy mum lays an egg in another bird's nest. When the egg hatches, it's the other bird that does all the hard work, raising the chick.

● The cuckoo manages to trick birds because her egg matches the other ones in the nest.

Which mother has her babies in prison?

While the female hornbill is laying her eggs in a hole in a tree, the male helps her to block up the door. But he leaves a hole for her beak so that he can feed her while she's stuck inside!

● Tree shrews are part-time mums. They leave their babies in the nest, only popping by to feed them every other day.

When does a puppy turn into a dog?

Every puppy is blind and helpless when it's born, but by the time it's two years old it will be fully grown. All pups are roughly the same size when they're born, whatever type of dog they are. So it takes smaller breeds less time to finish growing up!

2 By six weeks, the puppy is starting to explore. It plays with its brothers and sisters, and enjoys a tumble!

1 At about two weeks, the puppy's eyes and ears open. It will begin walking soon.

● A baby wildebeest runs before it even walks! The youngster trots along beside its mother just five minutes after it's born.

When does a tiger cub leave home?

A mother tiger looks after her cubs until they're about two years old. But then she has another litter, and ignores the older cubs. It's not really cruel – the two-year-olds are grown-up now, and it's about time they took care of themselves.

3 By the time it is fully grown, the dog is strong and active. Good food and exercise will help it to stay fit.

● Most insects change shape as they grow. A beetle starts life as a wriggly larva. Then it turns into a pupa. It may not look like it's doing much, but inside the hard skin the insect is changing fast. When it crawls out, it's a fully-grown beetle.

Larva　　**Pupa**　　**Beetle**

What does an insect feel with its feelers?

Luna moth

Insects use their feelers to taste and smell – the longer the feelers, the better. Some insects also use their feelers like fingers, to check things out by touching.

● The male luna moth's feelers are long and feathery. He uses them to smell out female moths many kilometres away.

● A male insect's feelers are often larger than a female's. They help him to sniff her out at mating time.

● The cockchafer beetle always fans out its feelers before it flies. They tell it which way the wind is blowing.

Banded longhorn beetle

Cockchafer beetle

● The banded longhorn beetle doesn't just have stripey feelers. The rest of it is blue and black, too!

Ant

Which insect tastes with its toes?

Most insects taste food with their mouths, as we do, but the honey bee can taste with its feet as well. It only needs to land on a flower to sample the dish of the day!

● Spiders have eight eyes, but they're very short-sighted!

Which insect listens with its legs?

The long-horned grasshopper has ears on both its front legs. Its ears don't look like ours, of course. They're tiny holes with skin stretched over the top – a bit like miniature drums.

Why do moths flutter around lamps?

When moths fly at night, they use the Moon and stars to find their way. A bright light just confuses them. They circle and crash into it, and may even burn their wings on the hot bulb.

Why do glow-worms glow?

A glow-worm glows to attract a mate. It flashes out a message to other glow-worms in the neighbourhood. Then the glow-worm sits back and waits for a reply!

● The female North American firefly tells lies. She flashes the signal of a different kind of firefly, and when the male comes near, she eats him!

How do grasshoppers play the violin?

The meadow grasshopper plays its body like a violin. It uses its back leg like a bow, scraping it against its wing to make a loud chirruping sound. On a warm summer's day, you may have a whole orchestra in your garden!

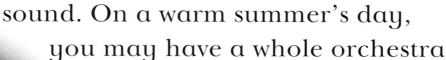

● Death-watch beetles like to munch through the floorboards, and they attract a mate by tapping their jaws. People once thought this knocking sound was a sign that someone in the house was about to die.

How do mosquitoes hum?

Female mosquitoes hum by beating their wings at up to 1,000 times a second. They do this to attract a mate. The hum has a different effect on people, though. They rush to put on their anti-mosquito cream!

● The world's loudest insect is the cicada. You can hear it over 500 metres away – that's about the length of five football pitches!

Which ants live in a tent?

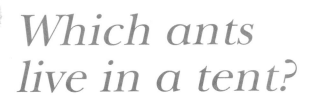

Weaver ants sew leaves together to make tents for themselves, and they use their larvae as needles and thread! Each ant holds a young grub in its mouth, and pokes it through the edges of two leaves. The grub makes a sticky, silky thread, which stitches the two leaves firmly together.

Whose house has a trapdoor?

The trapdoor spider's burrow has a door with a silk hinge which can open and shut. The spider hides inside, waiting for passing insects. When it hears one, it flings up the trapdoor, and grabs its victim.

● Many creepy-crawlies make their homes in your home. Ants, spiders, moths, centipedes and houseflies all like to live indoors.

Whose nest is paper thin?

The paper wasp's nest has paper walls. It makes the paper by chewing up strips of wood, which it tears from plants or old fence posts! It spreads the mixture in thin layers to build the nest.

● A tent caterpillar spins a shady silk canopy, and shelters under it while it feeds.

● Termites are champion builders, and make mud nests up to four times taller than a man. They need the room — as many as 5 million termites may be living inside!

Which cave is lit by insects?

There's no need to take a torch when you visit the magical Glowworm Grotto in New Zealand's Waitomo Cave. Its roof is lit by thousands of tiny glowworms that sparkle and twinkle like tiny, blue fairy-lights.

● The famous New Zealand opera singer, Kiri Te Kanawa, once gave a concert in another part of the Waitomo Cave, called the Cathedral.

Why are cave fish blind?

These fish are cave dwellers, and like other creatures that spend their whole lives deep underground, they don't need sight because they live in total darkness. Instead of sight, cave fish have special nerve endings in their skin which help them 'feel' their way about and track down food.

Cave fish

Which insects feed on bat droppings?

Bat droppings, or guano, are a rich source of food for cave minibeasts such as cockroaches, flies and millipedes. In their turn, these creatures are snapped up by centipedes, crickets and spiders, which are then hunted by larger cave animals such as bats and birds.

● The olm is an amphibian which has adapted to life in the dark zone of a cave. It has pale pink skin and lives in cave streams.

Centipede

Cricket

Harvestman

Olm

● Unlike their noisy relatives above ground, cave crickets don't chirrup.

Which dragon lives under water?

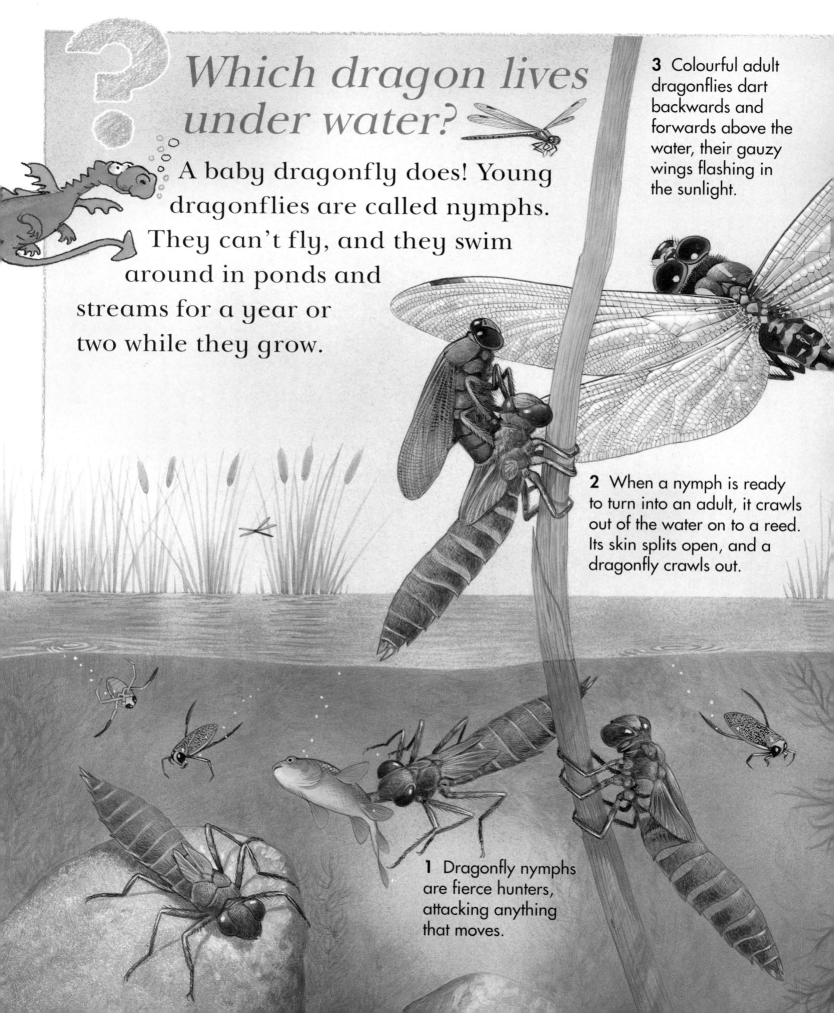

A baby dragonfly does! Young dragonflies are called nymphs. They can't fly, and they swim around in ponds and streams for a year or two while they grow.

3 Colourful adult dragonflies dart backwards and forwards above the water, their gauzy wings flashing in the sunlight.

2 When a nymph is ready to turn into an adult, it crawls out of the water on to a reed. Its skin splits open, and a dragonfly crawls out.

1 Dragonfly nymphs are fierce hunters, attacking anything that moves.

Which bug does the backstroke?

The greater water boatman spends all day lying on its back under the surface of the water, rowing along with its back legs. It must get tired of looking at the sky!

● The swamp spider loves fishing. It dabbles its feet in the water as bait for tiny fish. When they start to nibble its toes, it grabs them!

● The diving beetle's larvae are called a water tigers, and they're fierce enough to kill a fish!

● The water spider makes an underwater tent of silk. To stop the tent floating away, the spider anchors it with silk guy-ropes.

Which is the biggest reptile?

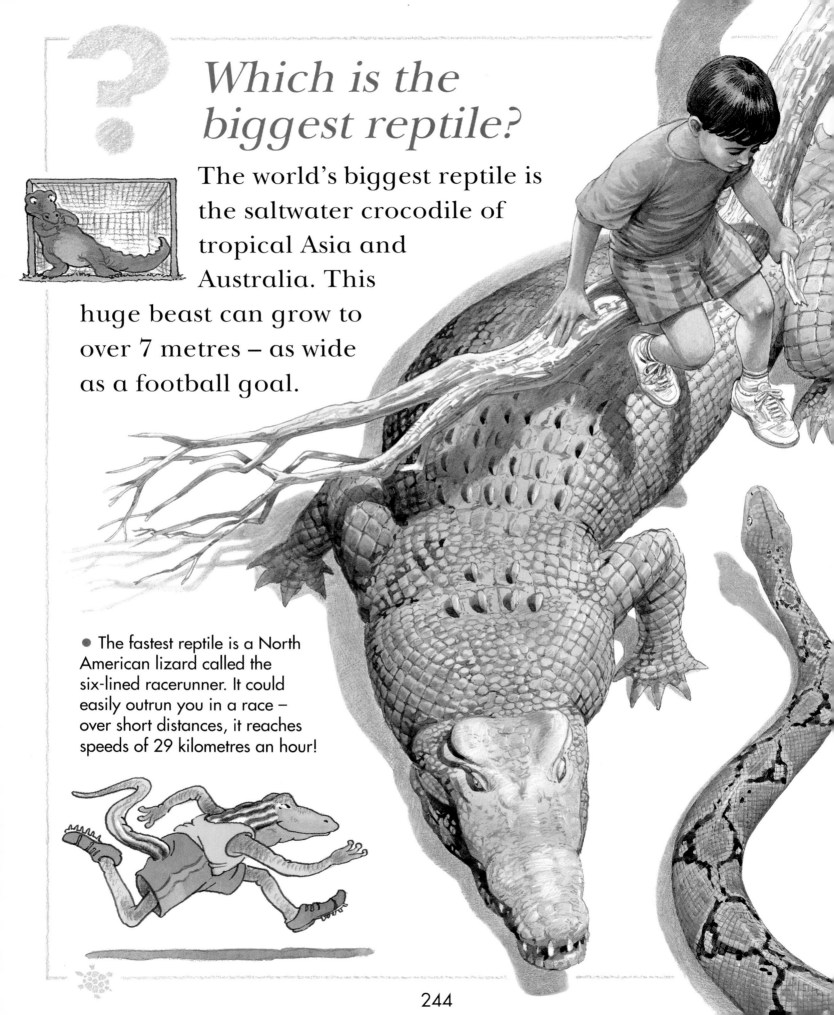

The world's biggest reptile is the saltwater crocodile of tropical Asia and Australia. This huge beast can grow to over 7 metres – as wide as a football goal.

● The fastest reptile is a North American lizard called the six-lined racerunner. It could easily outrun you in a race – over short distances, it reaches speeds of 29 kilometres an hour!

Which reptile lives the longest?

Tortoises can live to a ripe old age. The oldest one ever known lived to be 152 years old! But this might not be a record – there could be even older tortoises in the wild.

- The most spectacular reptiles have been dead for over 65 million years. They were the dinosaurs, the prehistoric relatives of today's reptiles.

- The smallest reptile is a tiny gecko lizard from the West Indies. It measures 3.5 centimetres from nose to tail, and would fit inside a book of matches with room to spare.

Which is the biggest snake?

The biggest snake is the anaconda of South America, which grows up to 10 metres – that's as long as a bus. The reticulated python is another whopper, but although it's as long as the anaconda, it's not as heavy.

245

How do lizards move in a hurry?

Some lizards find they can move much more quickly if they run on just two legs instead of on all fours. When something disturbs a crested water dragon and gives it a fright, it likes to make a speedy getaway. So the lizard stands up, pushes on its powerful back legs and hurries off just as fast as its legs will carry it.

How do snakes move without legs?

Snakes manage very well without legs. One of the ways they move is by throwing their bodies into zigzags. By pushing back against stones, they force themselves forward. Many snakes are good swimmers and tree-climbers, some burrow underground, and others even glide through the air.

- Geckos can walk upside down, thanks to tiny hairs on their feet. They have up to 150,000 hooked hairs on each toe. These stick like Velcro to whatever they touch – even a slippery pane of glass!

- Tortoises are never in a hurry. Most of them would take three hours or more to cross a football field.

How do crocodiles swim without fins?

Crocodiles may not have fins like a fish, but they have a very powerful tail. By lashing it from side to side, the crocodiles use their tail to propel them through the water like an oar. The animals tuck in their legs very close to their body to make themselves as smooth and as streamlined as possible. That way they slip along incredibly fast.

How do rattlesnakes kill their prey?

An attacking rattlesnake is lightning fast. It opens its mouth wide, swings its fangs forwards, then bites to inject a deadly poison through them. Small victims die within seconds.

● Rattlesnakes are named for the rattling noise they make by shaking the tip of their tail.

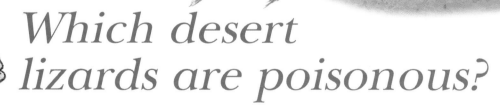

Which desert lizards are poisonous?

Hundreds of different lizards live in deserts, but only two are poisonous – the USA's gila monster and the Mexican beaded lizard. Don't worry, though. These lizards mainly use their poison to protect themselves from enemies, not to attack prey.

Why do scorpions have a sting in their tail?

Scorpions inject poison through their tails, but only if they're really cheesed off. Usually, they just use their claws to catch and kill prey. Scorpions have small eyes and don't see all that well, so they usually track prey using their senses of touch and smell instead.

● The chuckwalla lizard protects itself from enemies by squeezing into a crack in the rock and puffing its body up with air. It's as hard to pull out as a cork from a bottle.

● Scorpions eat insects and spiders mainly, but large scorpions will eat lizards and mice.

249

Do reptiles have skin like ours?

A reptile's skin is quite tough and horny, more like our fingernails than our skin. On snakes and lizards, most of the skin is covered with small scales that overlap one another. But crocodiles and turtles have an even tougher skin, with hard plates rather than scales.

● Snakes don't feel slimy. They're dry, cool and pleasant to touch.

● A reptile's scaly skin holds in water, and stops the animal from drying out. This is useful if you live in the desert, as many lizards do.

● A snake's old skin begins to split at the lips. The snake wriggles out head first, turning the skin inside out as it goes. The skin often comes off in one piece, in a perfect snake shape.

Why do snakes shed their skin?

Like your old clothes, a snake's skin wears out and needs replacing – often in a bigger size. So from three to seven times a year, the old skin splits open and peels off, and – hey presto! – there's a brand-new skin waiting underneath.

● In times of danger, the armadillo lizard turns into an armoured ball. It rolls on its back, grips its tail in its mouth and hides its soft belly behind a wall of scales and spines.

Why do some lizards have horns and spikes?

Horns and spikes are a good way of protecting an animal. Like a strong suit of armour, they make a lizard look fierce – and they also make a prickly mouthful for any animal that tries to attack.

How could a bonfire save elephants?

The President of Kenya once set fire to 12 tonnes of elephant tusks, worth over £1,500,000. The tusks had been taken away from poachers. By burning them, Kenya was saying to the world that it thought buying and selling ivory was wrong. It was hoping to persuade other countries to stop the trade in ivory and do more to protect the elephants.

Who grabs robber crabs?

Robber crabs live on islands in the Pacific and Indian Oceans. Some grow to one metre across. They are hunted for food and made into souvenirs for tourists.

● At 180 cm long, the Chinese giant salamander is the largest salamander in the world. So many people enjoy eating it that it has become endangered.

Why would leopards rather not be spotted?

Some people like to wear coats made of beautiful, spotted leopard skins. Others hunt big cats because they find it an exciting sport. If the leopards had a voice, they might say they'd rather have a plain skin that nobody wanted to wear – or else be harder to see in the first place.

When do parrots make bad pets?

Parrots make bad pets when they are born to be wild. Every year thousands of parrots are taken from their natural home to other countries in tiny, cramped boxes. Many die before they even get there, many more soon after.

THIS WAY UP

THE TRULY WILD PET SHOP

• An animal that is taken from its natural home is less likely to survive than one that is born and bred by people. If you want a pet, make sure that it isn't a wild animal.

• Spix's macaws have been highly prized as pets. Today there are only 31 left, of which just one lives in the wild. If he doesn't breed with the female that has been released near to him, his species will be extinct in the wild.

● It is a good idea to find out how large your pet will become before you buy it. People are often surprised when the small pet they took home grows into a monster!

Who carries a chameleon in a suitcase?

Holiday-makers have been caught with chameleons in their suitcases. It's against the law to take endangered animals from one country to another. These people wanted to smuggle the lizards home.

● Chimps, macaques and tamarins are often kept by scientists who test their new medicines on them. Some people say this has to be done to make sure that medicines are safe for humans. Others say it is cruel and should be stopped.

255

Which bird is a giant?

The ostrich is the biggest living bird. From top to toe it's over 2.5 metres tall – that's about as high as the ceiling! And it's heavy, too, weighing about the same as a Shetland pony!

● The biggest flying bird is the wandering albatross. From wingtip to wingtip it's as long as a family car!

● The ostrich can't fly. But it can run from danger at up to 72 kilometres per hour – that's faster than a racehorse.

Ostrich

Which bird flies fastest?

Eider duck

The eider duck can fly along at up to 100 kilometres per hour. But the real record-breaker is the peregrine falcon. It swoops down on its prey at over 200 kilometres per hour, making it the fastest animal on Earth.

● The fastest swimmer is the gentoo penguin. It can race through the water at up to 27 kilometres per hour – that's three times faster than the fastest person.

Peregrine falcon

Which is the smallest bird?

● The African kori bustard is the heaviest flying bird. Sometimes it even has trouble getting off the ground!

In tropical rainforests, many of the birds are smaller than the butterflies. The Cuban bee hummingbird is probably the smallest of all. It's about as big as the eye of an ostrich – and can perch on the end of a pencil.

Why are birds special?

Birds are not the only animals with wings, the only ones that lay eggs, or the only ones with beaks. But they are the only creatures in the whole wide world that have feathers.

● Birds aren't the only animals to fly. Bats do, too – and they're mammals.

● Birds aren't the only animals to have a beak. The duck-billed platypus does, too.

● Birds aren't the only animals to lay eggs. Tortoises and other reptiles do, too.

● All birds have wings, but not all of them can fly. Some creep, hop, or run along the ground; others swim like seals in the sea.

● There are 30 birds in the world for every man, woman and child.

Which birds have scales?

All of them! Birds' feet and legs are covered with scaly skin, just like the skin of snakes and lizards. That's why you never see birds wearing shoes and socks! But the scales don't stop there. A bird's feathers may seem soft to the touch, but they're made of tough, horny stuff – just like scales.

Why do birds fly?

Flying is a great way to escape from enemies. With a few flaps of its wings, a bird can get to a safe perch well out of the reach of a hungry cat! Being able to fly also helps birds to move quickly from one feeding ground to another, and to catch insects that buzz through the air.

● The handsome roller bird is a true acrobat. When chasing insects, it performs somersaults in the air.

How do birds fly?

The usual way for a bird to fly is to flap its wings up and down. This pushes it through the air, just as oars push a boat through the water. But it's hard work, so some birds save energy by gliding. Once they've built up speed, they spread out their wings, and let breezy air currents carry them along.

● Like planes, birds need to be strong but light. To keep their weight down, they have hollow or paper-thin bones.

● Hummingbirds are the only birds that can fly backwards. They can also fly forwards, sideways and upside-down!

● The common swift spends nearly its whole life in the air. It even sleeps on the wing!

z z z z z z z z z

z z z z

How many feathers does a bird have?

The bigger a bird is, the more feathers it has. A hummingbird has about 900 feathers, while a swan has 25,000! Feathers come in all different shapes and sizes. Soft downy feathers keep the bird warm, others keep it waterproof in the rain, and the strongest feathers give it the power to fly.

● Birds have long tail feathers, smooth wing and body feathers, and fluffy down feathers. Down is warmer than fur – it's like a bird's woolly underwear.

Tail feathers

Golden pheasant

Pheasant

Body feathers

Parrot

African grey parrot

Down feather

Goose

Scarlet macaw

Guinea fowl

● Every wing feather is made up of hundreds of hair-like strands. These zip together with tiny hooks to make a smooth, strong blade.

Why are vultures bald?

Vultures are messy eaters. They feed on dead animals, pushing their heads right inside the bodies to tear into the meat. If they had head feathers, they'd get dirty and sticky, and would be almost impossible to clean. That's why vultures are much better off being bald.

● Feathers work so hard that they wear out. The bird grows a new set each year and the old ones gradually fall out. This is called moulting.

Wing feathers

Parrot

Seagull

Macaw

Flamingo

Turkey

● Before pens were invented, people wrote with quills. These were large feathers, sharpened at the end and dipped in ink.

Who eats with giant tweezers?

A hungry toucan pushes leaves apart with its big, long beak. Then the bird uses the tip of its beak very delicately, like tweezers, to pick fruit off the branch. Next it tosses the fruit up in the air and snaps it up as it falls.

● The Galápagos woodpecker finch is the only bird to use a fork! It grasps a twig in its beak to poke out insects from holes in the trees.

...a pair of pliers?

Crossbills feed on the seeds inside pine cones, and they have a very special beak to prise them out. The top half of the beak twists over the bottom half. This helps the birds to get a good grip and force the cones open.

● The sword-billed hummingbird's beak is longer than its body. It's like a straw to suck nectar from deep inside a flower.

...a sieve?

The inside of a flamingo's beak acts like a sieve. As the bird slurps up a beakful of water, it pours out through the holes, leaving behind a tasty mouthful of tiny water creatures.

● The frigate bird is a real pirate. When other seabirds catch fish, it attacks them, and steals their booty!

...and a spear?

The anhinga is a waterbird that feeds on frogs and fish. It stands stock-still in the water for hours, waiting for some dinner to swim by. When it spies a catch, it spears its prey quick as a flash with its long, dagger-like beak.

● The secretary bird of Africa hunts with its feet! It catches snakes in its claws and stamps them to death.

Which is the biggest eagle?

The harpy eagle is bigger than a Great Dane, and is the largest and most powerful of the eagles. It lives in the rainforests of South America, where it chases monkeys through the trees, grabbing them with its deadly claws!

● An eagle's feet are deadly weapons. Its toes are strong enough to crush its prey, and its claws are razor-sharp.

● Birds are some of the best fishermen in the world. When an osprey dives into the water, it can catch fish more than half its own size.

● Vultures sometimes eat so much that they can't take off after their meal.

Which birds have sneaky wings?

Most owls hunt at night, swooping down silently on rabbits, mice and other tasty prey. The hunters have special fringed wing feathers, which can beat the air without making a sound. That way, their prey doesn't hear them coming, and has no time to escape!

● The Everglade kite lives on water snails. Its hooked beak is just the right shape to winkle a snail from its shell.

● Owls eat their prey whole. Later, they cough up all the bones and fur in a neat little sausage-shaped pellet.

Why does a budgie cock its head?

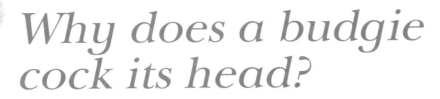

A budgie's eyes are on the side of its head so that it can see all around. But seeing things close up is harder work. The bird has to cock its head and aim a special viewer in the middle of its eye – a bit like when you aim your camera to take a photo.

● The woodcock has the most extraordinary eyes. Without moving its head, it can see what's going on in front, behind and even above.

Which bird steers with its ears?

The South American oilbird makes its nest deep in a cave. It can't see in the darkness so, as it flies, the oilbird makes non-stop clicking noises, which echo when they bounce off the cave walls. By listening to where the echoes come from, the oilbird knows exactly where the cave walls are.

- Ducks have a pair of see-through eyelids that protect their eyes when they dive. The eyelids are just like swimming goggles, helping ducks to see under water.

Which bird sniffs all night?

The New Zealand kiwi hunts at night, using its nose to sniff out worms, insects and other tasty titbits. Unlike other birds' nostrils, a kiwi's are at the end of its long beak. To find itself some dinner, all it has to do is stick its beak in the soil and take a jolly good sniff!

- The honeyguide feeds on beeswax. When it's sniffed out a bees' nest, it sometimes leads people to the spot and waits for them to break the nest open. Then the people can eat the honey and the honeyguide gets the wax.

Who's the best-dressed bird?

Male birds of paradise grow beautiful lacy feathers during the breeding season. When a female comes by, all the males hang upside-down to show off their stunning plumage. It's a beauty contest, and the female picks the bird with the finest feathers to be her mate!

Do all birds sing?

Just over half of all birds sing, but the rest are far from silent. Geese honk, owls hoot, gulls mew, and the Australian kookaburra seems to laugh. It's mostly male birds that sing – either to attract a mate or to warn other males to clear off their patch.

● In some New York houses, parrots are trained as burglar alarms! They let out a piercing shriek if someone breaks in.

● The male palm cockatoo attracts a mate by playing her a tune. He grasps a twig in one foot and uses it as a drumstick to beat a hollow log.

Which bird looks a fright?

If you scare a hawk-eagle, it'll probably scare you back! This bird has a crest of long feathers on its head. When it feels in danger, these feathers stand on end. This makes the eagle look look bigger and fiercer than it really is – with any luck, it will frighten away the enemy.

Which is the cleverest builder?

The male weaver bird has to prove he's a good nest-builder before he can win a mate. He hangs from a branch, weaving long strips of grass into a hollow ball. If his nest is good enough, the female will line it with feathers. If not, he has to start all over again!

● Many birds spend the night huddled together in sheltered spots. It helps them to keep warm, especially in winter. This is called roosting.

Which nest has central heating?

The Australian mallee fowl lays her eggs inside a big pile of leaves. As they rot, the leaves give off heat and keep the eggs nice and warm. Every day the father checks the nest with his beak. If it's too hot, he makes a hole to cool it down.

272

● Mockingbirds on the Galápagos Islands snatch hair from people's heads to line their nests.

Who lives in a city by the sea?

For many seabirds, a cliff is the perfect place to nest – it's out of reach for hunters and handy for fishing. Thousands of birds lay their eggs on the narrow ledges or nest in cracks in the rocks. With all those birds fighting for space, it's like a kind of city – crowded, smelly and very noisy!

When do birds have teeth?

Inside the egg, a baby chick grows a little tooth on its beak. When the chick is ready to hatch, it uses this tooth to chip away at the eggshell from the inside. The baby bird never needs its tooth again, so it drops off soon after hatching.

● A kingfisher's nest is a stinking mess of fish bones and droppings. As soon as they leave the nest, the chicks dive in the river for a good wash!

1 A baby bird chips a hole in the shell.

2 More holes make a dotted line.

Which eggs look like pebbles?

If you're walking on a pebbly beach in the spring, watch where you're putting your feet! Some of those round, speckly pebbles may be a plover's eggs. Plovers make their nests on open ground, but their eggs are perfectly hidden – because they look just like pebbles.

● Baby birds are hungry little things. A mother wren may feed her young hundreds of times a day!

Who starts life with a jump?

Mallard ducks often nest in holes in the trees, so their ducklings hatch high off the ground. How do they get down? Easy! When their mother calls, they jump out and tumble to the ground. They're so light that they don't need a parachute, and they all land safe and sound.

● Flamingo chicks feed on a runny food made by their parents. It's rather like mammals' milk – except that it's red not white!

3 The end of the shell breaks away...

4 ...and a damp duckling wriggles out.

5 Now the baby bird is ready to explore.

● A duck egg hatches about four weeks after it has been laid. Hatching can take anything from an hour or two to a whole day!

Why do geese take a winter holiday?

Brent geese fly from one land to another when the seasons change. This is called migration. The birds spend summer in the far north, raising their chicks on grasses and other plants. But if they stayed on in winter, they'd starve! So each autumn they fly to warmer lands.

● It gets so cold in Antarctica that some penguins migrate northwards to South America. They don't fly, of course – they swim!

How do they know when to go?

In autumn, the days grow cooler and shorter. This is a signal to migrating birds that it will soon be time to leave. They eat extra food, fattening themselves up for the journey ahead. Then on a fine day they gather together and fly away.

● The tiny rufous hummingbird spends summer in Alaska and winter in Mexico. That's a round trip of at least 9,600 kilometres!

How do they find their way?

Scientists aren't sure how migrating birds find their way. Some birds seem to know which way to go, as if they had a compass inside them. Others may steer by the sun, moon and stars. And older birds probably remember landmarks, such as rivers and hills.

● Flying long distances uses up lots of energy. Weary birds stop off on the way to rest and fill up with food.

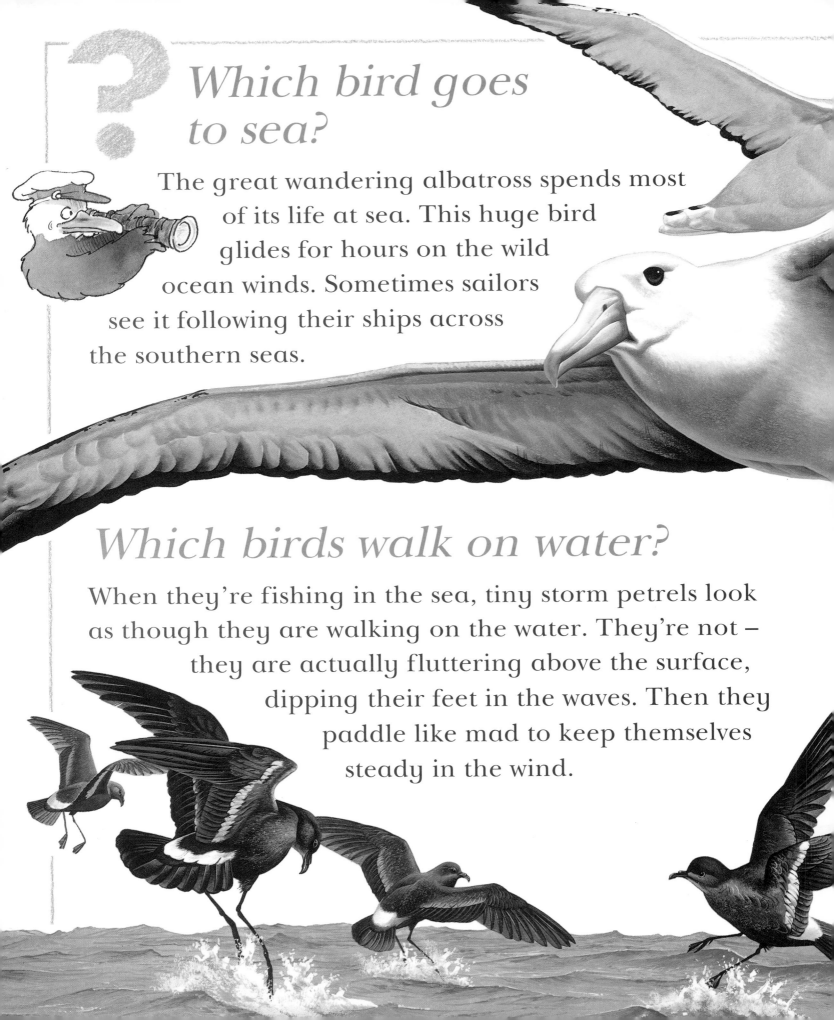

Which bird goes to sea?

The great wandering albatross spends most of its life at sea. This huge bird glides for hours on the wild ocean winds. Sometimes sailors see it following their ships across the southern seas.

Which birds walk on water?

When they're fishing in the sea, tiny storm petrels look as though they are walking on the water. They're not – they are actually fluttering above the surface, dipping their feet in the waves. Then they paddle like mad to keep themselves steady in the wind.

Which bird wears a crash helmet?

Gannets are wonderful divers. They dive into the sea from a great height to catch their fishy dinner. But smacking into the water could give them a headache. That's why they have a thick bony skull like a crash helmet, to protect them when they hit the water.

Who likes to paddle in the mud?

Wading birds love the sticky mud at the mouth of a river. Huge flocks of them paddle about in it for hours, sticking in their beaks to hunt out worms, crabs and crunchy shellfish.

● A puffin can carry home as many as 40 fish in its mouth. Little ridges along the beak give it an extra-firm grip.

How do penguins stand the cold?

● Penguin chicks snuggle between their parent's feet to keep warm.

The emperor penguin is the only animal to survive the Antarctic winter on land. Penguins have a thick coat of feathers, and an even thicker coat of fat under their skin. Even with their double overcoats, the birds huddle in huge crowds to keep warm in the biting winds.

● The ptarmigan lives in the far north. During the summer, its feathers are brown. But every autumn, it grows a new coat of white feathers – an excellent disguise to fool hunters in the snow.

● The snowy owl is a hardy bird. To keep out the Arctic chill, it has extra-thick feathers on its legs and feet – just like a warm pair of leggings.

- The male sandgrouse will fly hundreds of kilometres to a water hole to get a drink for his chicks. He soaks up water in his feathers, and lets the chicks suck it all out.

- In hot deserts, nesting birds have to shade their eggs from the sun. If they didn't, the eggs would cook, killing the young chicks inside.

How do desert birds stand the heat?

The tiny elf owl lives in the hot deserts of America. Like many other desert animals, it rests during the day, out of reach of the scorching sun. A nest hole in a saguaro cactus makes the perfect hiding place. The cactus's thick, juicy walls help to keep out the heat, making a cool shelter for a sleepy owl.

Plants

What is a plant?

Plants are living things. They come in all shapes and sizes, from tiny waterweeds to towering trees. Plants are different from animals in one very important way – they can make food for themselves from sunlight. Animals can't do this. They depend on plants for their food.

Where do plants grow?

There are about 380,000 different kinds of plants on Earth, and they grow just about everywhere – in fields and forests, deserts and mountains. Apart from air, the two things plants need are sunlight and water, so you won't find them in places that are completely dark or dry.

● All the food in the world starts with plants. You may eat eggs, meat and cheese but, without plants, no chicken or cow could produce these foods!

Are plants really alive?

Plants are just as alive as you are. They need air, food and water to grow, and they can make lots of new plants like themselves. This proves that they're alive. Things like stones and rocks don't feed, grow or have young because they're not alive.

● Corals and sea-anemones may look like plants, but they are imposters. In fact, they're animals!

Why do trees have leaves?

Like all plants, trees need their leaves to stay alive. Leaves are a tree's food factories. They contain a sticky green stuff called chlorophyll. The chlorophyll uses water, sunlight and carbon dioxide in the air to make a sugary food. The food is then carried to every part of the tree in a sweet and sticky juice called sap.

• If you've ever chewed a blade of grass, you'll know how sweet sap tastes. Hungry young caterpillars think so, too. That's why they eat leaves!

Why do some trees lose their leaves in autumn?

Big green leaves are useful in spring and summer. They make food while the sun shines and the days are long. When the days get shorter, there's less time for making food and the tree must live off its food reserves. Rather than feed their leaves too, some trees shed their leaves in autumn.

● The way plants make food in their leaves is called photosynthesis. During photosynthesis, plants take in carbon dioxide from the air. And they give out oxygen – the gas we all need to survive.

Why do leaves change colour in autumn?

● We call plants that lose their leaves in the autumn deciduous. Evergreens have tough leaves that can survive the winter. The trees still lose their leaves, but not all at the same time.

It's the chlorophyll in a plant's leaves that makes them look green. But in autumn, the chlorophyll breaks down. Once the green colouring has gone, the leaves' other colours show through – beautiful shades of red, yellow and gold.

Why do roots grow so long?

Long roots fix a plant firmly in the ground so that it won't fall over on windy days. But roots do another job, too. By spreading out far and wide, they can suck up water and goodness from all the soil around. Then the roots send the water up the stem or trunk and into the leaves.

• In the strongest winds, a tree can sometimes be blown right over. Its roots are wrenched out of the ground as the tree falls down with a crash.

• A wild fig tree in South Africa grew roots 120 metres down into the soil. If it was put on the roof of a 40-storey office block, its roots would reach down to the ground.

• At the ends of the roots are tiny hairs, which burrow into the spaces between the lumps of soil.

● Sunflowers not only grow up towards the light, but their flowers follow the Sun! As the Sun appears to move across the sky through the day, the flower-heads turn to face it.

Why are stems so straight?

A plant needs to hold its leaves up to the sunshine, which it uses to make its food. Many plants grow tall, straight stems, so that they can beat their neighbours to the sunlight.

● Not all plants have straight stems. Some have stems that bend and curl, clambering their way over nearby plants as they climb up to the light.

What is a forest?

A forest is a large area of land covered by trees. Beneath the trees there are smaller plants, such as bushes and flowers. Living among the plants there are all sorts of animals – insects, birds and, in some forests, bigger creatures such as foxes or wild boars.

● A single tree in an oak forest is home to as many as 400 kinds of animal, from insects and spiders to birds and squirrels.

How do forests help us breathe?

Like other animals, we breathe in oxygen from the air and breathe out carbon dioxide. Trees help us because they take in carbon dioxide and give off lots of oxygen.

● In a single year, a forest of 400 trees gives off enough oxygen to keep at least 20 people breathing.

Which forests have the largest trees?

The redwood forests of California, USA, have the tallest trees. Redwoods grow to over 75 metres – that's higher than a 30-storey building!

● If left unfarmed, almost any field will turn slowly into a forest. Bushes take over from grass, and then trees take over from bushes.

Which plants grow in water?

The giant water lily grows in the lakes and rivers of South America. Its roots lie deep in the mud and its huge leaves float on the water's surface. This is the best place for catching the sun! Each leaf curls up at the rim so that it can push other leaves aside.

● The giant water lily's leaves grow on long, strong stems. On the underside of each leaf is a web of supporting veins. This makes the leaves so strong that a toddler could sit on one without sinking!

Which are the smallest plants?

Although some types of algae grow to be the most enormous plants, there are other algae so small you can only see them through a microscope. The very smallest float in lakes and oceans, and are called phytoplankton. They're so tiny that whales catch millions in every gulp!

● The leaves and roots of water plants give food and shelter to many animals. But they're also places where hunters can hide.

Which forests grow in the sea?

Huge forests of kelp grow off the coast of California in the United States. Kelp is a kind of seaweed that grips on to rocks, and sends long ribbon-like stems up through the water. Some of the stems can be 200 metres long – as long as eight swimming pools laid end to end.

● Not all water plants are rooted in the mud. Some seaweeds float in the water, thanks to pockets of air in their leaves – rather like their very own rubber rings!

Which plant traps a treat?

When an insect lands on a Venus flytrap, it gets a nasty surprise! It only has to brush against one tiny hair on an open leaf tip, to make the leaf snap tightly shut. There's no escape for the poor insect. The flytrap changes it into a tasty soup, which it slowly soaks up.

● The bladderwort is an underwater meat-eater. Along its leaves are bubble-shaped bags, which suck in tiny creatures as they paddle past.

● Did you know that flytraps can count? The first time an insect touches a hair on one of the leaf tips, the trap stays open. But if it touches it a second time, the trap snaps shut!

one, two, three...

FLY SOUP

...fools a fly?

Pitcher plants have unusual vase-shaped leaves that tempt insects with a sugar-sweet smell. But the leaves are slippery traps. When a fly lands on them, it loses its footing, slips inside the 'vase', and drowns in a pool of juice.

● Many meat-eating plants grow on wet, boggy ground where the soil is very poor. They need their juicy snacks for extra nourishment.

...snares a snack?

The sundew's leaves are covered in hairs, which sparkle with glue-like drops. When an insect lands on a leaf, it gets stuck fast. The more it struggles, the more it sticks. At last, the leaf folds over, traps the fly, and starts dissolving it into liquid food that it can drink up.

Why do plants have flowers?

Many plants have colourful, perfumed flowers that attract insects and other animals. The visitors feed on drops of sweet nectar inside the flower. As they feed, they pick up a fine yellow dust called pollen, which they carry to another flower. When the pollen rubs off on the second flower, that flower can start to make seeds.

● This plant is called hotlips – and no wonder! The lipstick-red markings on its leaves are a wonderful way to attract visitors to its tiny flower.

● Many trees and grasses spread their pollen on the wind. They don't need animal visitors, so they don't grow bright flowers.

● Pollinators, such as this bat, don't mean to get pollen all over themselves. But a cactus flower is shaped in such a way that the bat just can't help it!

Which flower fools a bee?

A bee orchid's flowers look and smell just like female bees. Male bees zoom to the flowers wanting to mate with them – but they've been tricked! The plant's just using them as postmen to deliver little packets of pollen to other orchids nearby.

● During the summer, the air can be so full of pollen that it makes many people sneeze. Poor things – they haven't got a cold, they've got hayfever.

Which is the smelliest flower?

The dead horse arum is well named – it stinks of rotten meat! But blowflies love it. These plump flies usually lay their eggs inside the rotting bodies of dead animals. They're fooled by the plant's rotten smell, and crawl inside it to lay their eggs, picking up pollen on the way.

Why is fruit so sweet and juicy?

● The cotton-top tamarin lives in the South American rainforest. It feeds mainly on fruit, especially delicious, juicy figs.

Plants make sweet, juicy fruits so that animals will eat them. Inside every fruit is one or more seeds. When an animal swallows the fruit, it swallows the seeds as well. These pass through its body, and fall out in its droppings. In such good soil, the seeds soon start to grow into new plants!

● You often see seeds floating through the air. Dandelion seeds grow their own fluffy parachutes. And sycamore seeds have wings, which spin them to the ground like tiny helicopters.

Which plant shoots from the hip?

The Mediterranean squirting cucumber has a special way of spreading its seeds. As the fruit grows, it fills with a slimy juice. Day by day, the fruit grows fuller and fuller until it bursts, flinging the seeds far out into the air.

Which seeds sail away?

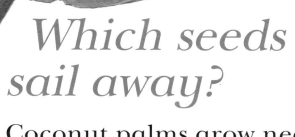

Coconut palms grow near the sea, so the ripe coconuts often fall into the water. Protected by their hard shell, they float out to sea. After several weeks or months, they are washed up on to a beach, where they sprout and start to grow.

● Fruits come in many different colours, but most animals seem to like red ones the best!

Which fruit gets forgotten?

Many animals feed on acorns, the fruits of the oak tree. Squirrels enjoy them so much that, every autumn, they bury some in the ground as a snack for when food is short in winter. The trouble is, the animals often forget where they've hidden their store, so when spring comes the young oaks start to grow.

When does a seed begin to grow?

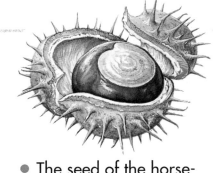

Inside every seed is the tiny beginning of a new plant. This starts to grow when the soil around the seed is warm and damp. At first, the baby plant feeds on a store of food inside the seed. But as soon as its first leaves open, it begins to make food for itself.

● The seed of the horse-chestnut tree has a tough brown coat. This rots away in the winter, and the young plant bursts through in the spring.

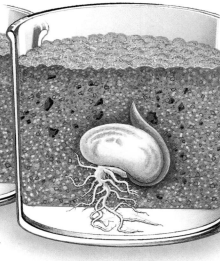

1 The bean seed swells with water, and splits open. A root starts to grow.

2 Tiny hairs grow out from the branches of the root.

3 A shoot appears. It grows up towards the light.

Do all plants grow from seeds?

Strawberry plants don't need seeds to produce new plants. They can send out side shoots, called runners. Where these touch the ground, roots begin to grow, then leaves and stems. In just a few weeks, there's a brand new plant!

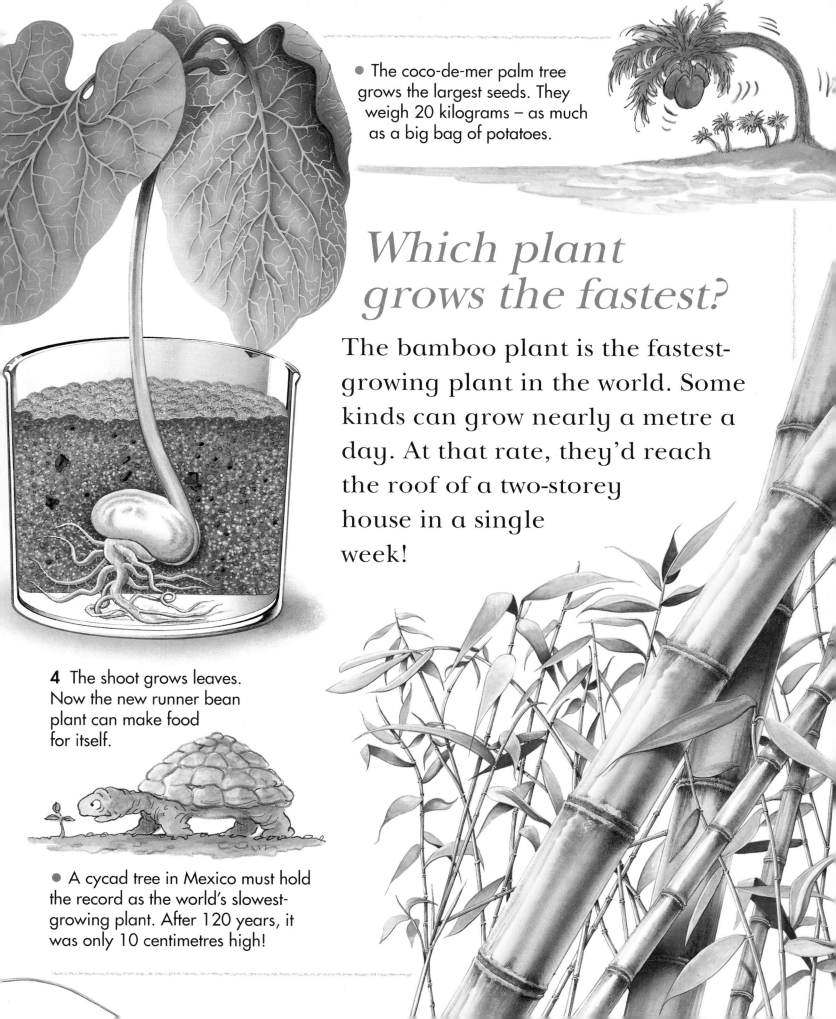

● The coco-de-mer palm tree grows the largest seeds. They weigh 20 kilograms – as much as a big bag of potatoes.

Which plant grows the fastest?

The bamboo plant is the fastest-growing plant in the world. Some kinds can grow nearly a metre a day. At that rate, they'd reach the roof of a two-storey house in a single week!

4 The shoot grows leaves. Now the new runner bean plant can make food for itself.

● A cycad tree in Mexico must hold the record as the world's slowest-growing plant. After 120 years, it was only 10 centimetres high!

Are fungi plants?

Fungi aren't really plants at all. They look like plants, and they grow in the same sort of places. But, unlike plants, they don't have leaves, stems or roots, and they don't make their food from sunlight. A fungus grows by soaking up food from dead animals and plants.

● Scientists have found over 100,000 different kinds of fungi – and there are probably many more. These tiny bright blue toadstools grow in New Zealand.

What puffs out of a puffball?

A puffball is a kind of fungus that looks like a large creamy ball. If you knock a ripe one, a cloud of dust puffs out of the top. This dust is really millions of tiny specks called spores. Spores do the same job as seeds. If they land in rich soil, they will grow into brand new puffballs.

● Did you know that the blue bits in some cheeses are a kind of fungus?

● There were plants on land long before there were animals. Some of the kinds that plant-eating dinosaurs ate are still around today.

Which are the oldest plants?

Soft mosses and tall ferns first appeared on land about 350 million years ago. But the very first plants appeared on Earth more than 3,000 million years earlier. They were tiny, microscopic plants called algae, which floated in the sea

● One kind of fungus not only feeds on dead animals, it kills them first! The tiny spores grow inside live ants, feeding on the juicy bits of their bodies. Soon, nothing is left but the ant's dry skeleton, with the toadstools growing out of it.

Why do trees have thorns?

Trees such as the acacia have thorns to keep plant-eating animals away, but they don't always work. Goats, camels and giraffes, for example, have tough lips and mouths and long, curling tongues to get round the thorns. The plants will have to come up with another trick!

● The leaves on the lowest branches of a holly tree are the prickliest, to stop animals nibbling them. Higher up, the leaves are out of reach, so they're a lot less spiny.

Why do stinging nettles sting?

Stinging is another way plants protect themselves. Each leaf on a nettle is covered with little hairs as sharp as glass. If an animal sniffs one, the hair pricks the animal's nose and injects a drop of painful poison – ouch! It won't stick around to eat that leaf!

Which plants look like pebbles?

● Milkweed is a poisonous plant, but the caterpillars of the monarch butterfly eat it and come to no harm. It even makes them poisonous – so they don't get eaten by birds.

Pebble plants grow in the desert in southern Africa. They have two fat, juicy leaves that any animal would love to eat. But the plant protects itself by blending in with the background. Its leaves are disguised to look so pebble-like that animals pass it by.

Which plants get a lift to the light?

In rainforests the tallest trees spread out their branches in the sunshine, making it shady down below. Because of this, some smaller plants don't get enough light. A group of plants called epiphytes have solved the problem by perching high on the branches of trees and growing up there instead.

Which plant has a private pool?

Bromeliads are epiphytes that grow high up on rainforest trees. They don't use roots to collect water – every time it rains, the plants catch drops of water in a pool in the middle of their leaves. The tiny pools are perfect for tree frogs to relax in, too!

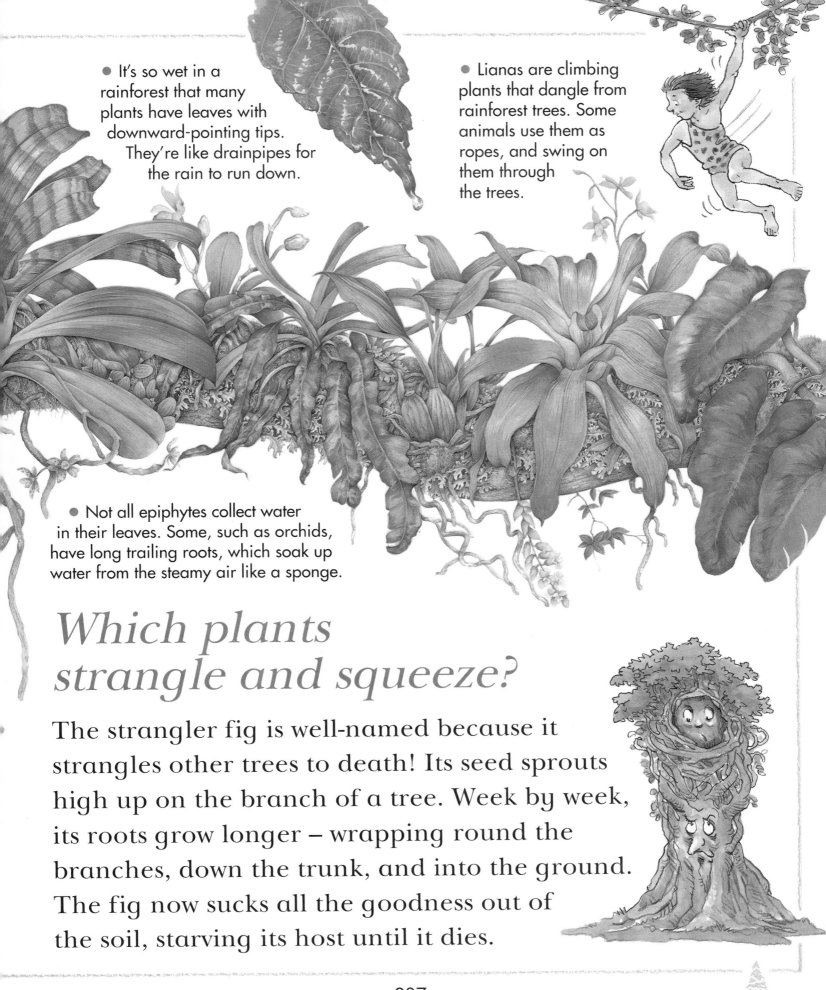

- It's so wet in a rainforest that many plants have leaves with downward-pointing tips. They're like drainpipes for the rain to run down.

- Lianas are climbing plants that dangle from rainforest trees. Some animals use them as ropes, and swing on them through the trees.

- Not all epiphytes collect water in their leaves. Some, such as orchids, have long trailing roots, which soak up water from the steamy air like a sponge.

Which plants strangle and squeeze?

The strangler fig is well-named because it strangles other trees to death! Its seed sprouts high up on the branch of a tree. Week by week, its roots grow longer – wrapping round the branches, down the trunk, and into the ground. The fig now sucks all the goodness out of the soil, starving its host until it dies.

Can plants grow in a desert?

Plants can grow in a desert, but they need special ways to survive. Cacti have spreading roots that slurp up any rain as soon as it falls. Then they take great care of the water, storing it inside their fat juicy stems. It may have to last them weeks, months or even years.

● Desert plants save lives! Many thirsty travellers have sucked life-saving water from the juicy flesh of a cactus.

Can you pick fruit in the desert?

Huge bunches of sweet, sticky dates dangle from palm trees, beside springs in the deserts of Africa and the Middle East. People have been picking the delicious fruit in these parts for more than 5,000 years.

● A gila woodpecker makes a cool nest for itself by carving out a hole in a cactus. When it leaves, there's a long queue of other birds who'd like to move in!

Can you find flowers in the desert?

Daisies, poppies and many other plants flower in the desert. The plants wither and die during the hot, dry months, but their seeds survive in the ground. When it rains, they soon spring into action. They grow into new plants and cover the dry desert with a beautiful carpet of flowers within a few weeks.

Which are the tastiest plants?

Spices are made from plants. They have such a strong smell and taste that we use them in cooking to give food a kick! After being harvested, most spices are dried, and then crushed to a powder that you can add to your food.

● Spices are made from different parts of plants. Pepper comes from berries, cinnamon from bark, and ginger from a root.

● Most spices come from plants which grow in tropical parts of the world. For hundreds of years, merchants have travelled around the world to buy spices at markets like this.

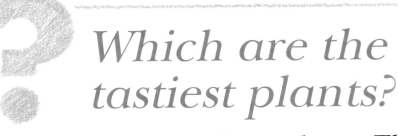

Why do carrot plants grow carrots?

A carrot is a tasty food – but it's not really meant for us! Carrot plants live for just two years. In the first year they make food, which they store in a fat orange root. They use up the food in the second year, while they're growing flowers and seeds – as long as the carrots haven't already been picked!

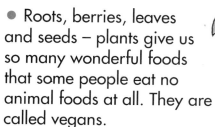

● Roots, berries, leaves and seeds – plants give us so many wonderful foods that some people eat no animal foods at all. They are called vegans.

Do people ever eat grass?

Wheat, rice, corn, barley, oats and rye are just some of the grasses that people eat all over the world. We don't eat the leaves like cows and other animals do. We harvest the seeds. Then we either eat them whole, or grind them into flour to make pasta, bread and other important foods.

● Scientists can improve seeds so that they grow into stronger, healthier plants. This helps farmers to grow bigger and better crops.

What are old plants good for?

Three hundred million years ago, there were huge forests of trees and ferns. As the plants died, they fell into muddy swamps and were buried in the mud. Slowly, over millions of years, the plants were pressed down and turned into a black rock called coal. Coal is a fuel. We burn it in power stations to make electricity.

● The coal we burn today comes from plants that grew before there were even dinosaurs!

● Shampoos, perfumes, bath oils and creams are all made from sweet-smelling plants. That's how you smell so sweet!

● In some parts of the world, people run their cars on fuels made from corn, potato and sugarcane plants.

● The corks that seal bottles of wine are made from the bark of the cork oak tree.

● Many of the medicines we buy at the chemist's are made from plants.

What are plants good for today?

Today's plants are still giving us the food and oxygen we need to survive. They also help us to make lots of useful things, such as paper, clothes and medicines. Every year, scientists discover new plants, and new ways to use them. So let's protect our plants.

● All sorts of useful things are made from rubber. It comes from the sticky juices of the rubber tree.

Flax

Cotton

● Cotton cloth is made from the soft hairs that surround the cotton plant's seeds. Linen is made from the stems of the flax plant.

Index

V

vegans 311
Venice 75, 80
Venus flytraps 294–295
Venus (goddess of love) 66
Venus (planet) 130, 134
vertebrates 220
Vietnam 112
Vikings 75, 207
volcanic ash 71, 196, 198, 199
volcanoes 31, 154, 166–167, 173, 191, 196–199, 201
Vulcan 196
vultures 263, 267

W

wading birds 279
wadis 161

water 71, 84, 96, 99, 132, 135, 144, 160–161, 308
water boatmen 243
water lillies 292
waterspouts 186, 187
waves 174, 184, 200–201
weapons 64–65, 78, 79
weather 144–145, 180–189, 198, 204–207
weaver ants 238
weaver birds 272–273
whales 32, 212–213, 292
wheatfields 110
wildebeest 232
Wills, William 98
wind 156, 180–186, 188, 206
windmills 83
Winter Olympics 94, 114
wolves 60, 153

woodcocks 268
woodpecker finches 264
woodpeckers 309
'World of the Ice Giants' 173
writing 12, 82, 263

Y

Yoruba 81
yurts 105

Z

zebras 216
Zeus 55, 58

Acknowledgements

I Wonder Why **series designer:** David West Children's Books
Additional design: Joanne Brown

Contributing authors: Andrew Charman, Jackie Gaff, Anita Ganeri, Rosie Greenwood, Fiona Macdonald Amanda O'Neill, Steve Parker, Philip Steele, Carole Stott, Jenny Wood

Contributing consultants: Andrew Branson; Michael Chinery; Department of Egyptian Antiquities, British Museum; Paul Hillyard; Dr David Hughes, Reader in Astronomy, Sheffield University; Keith Lye; Jane Parker, Steve Parker, Dr Paul Roberts, Louise Schofield;

Contributing illustrators: Andrew Beckett (Garden Studio) 286–287; John Butler 222–223; Joanne Cowne 232–233; Peter Dennis (Linda Roger's Associates) 64–65, 68–69, 106–107, 244–245, 252–253, 310–311; Bill Donohoe 198; Richard Draper 296–297; James Field 20–33, 98–99, 102–103, 120–121; Chris Forsey 48–49, 74–75, 94–97, 108–109, 110–111, 124–125, 138–149, 152–155, 168–169, 170–171, 178–181, 184–187, 194–197, 204–207, 236–237, 294–295, 312–313; Terry Gabbey (AFA) 112–113; Luigi Galante (Virgil Pomfret Agency) 40–41, 70–71, 104–105; Lindsay Graham 216–217; Andrew Harland (SGA) 18–19; Nick Harris (Virgil Pomfret Agency) 76–77, 80–81, 84–85, 88–89; Stephen Holmes (Eunice McMullen) 210–213, 220–221, 224–225, 238–239; Christa Hook (Linden Artists) 78–79; Adam Hook (Linden Artists) 44–45, 82–83; Biz Hull (Artist Partners) 288–289; Ian Jackson 118–119, 214–215, 218–219, 284–285, 298–299, 302–303, 308–309; Mike Lacey (SGA) 12–13, 35–37, 100–101, 114–117, 156–157, 162, 168–169, 172–173, 193, 199; Terence Lambert 254–255; Adrian Lascom (Garden Studio) 234–235; Simon Mendez 202–203; David Mitcheson 86; Nicki Palin 42–43, 46–47, 62–63, 230–231, 246–247, 250–251, 292–293, 306–307; Maurice Pledger (Bernard Thornton) 242–243; Bryan Poole 150–151, 226–227; Sebastian Quigley (Linden Artists) 126–129, 132–135; Claudia Saraceni 66–67; Sarah Smith (SGA) 14–15; Tony Smith (Virgil Pomfret Agency) 90–91; Roger Stewart 182; Steven Sweet 158–159, 164–165; Mike Taylor (SGA) 166–167, 174–175, 183, 188–191, 240–241; Ian Thompson 130–131; Ross Walton (SGA) 16–17, 34, 163; David Wright 228–229, 248–249; Dan Wright 300–301, 304–305.